MW01038322

LOSING

OUR

RELIGION

LOSING
OUR
RELIGION

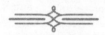

An Altar Call for
Evangelical America

Russell Moore

SENTINEL

Sentinel
An imprint of Penguin Random House LLC
penguinrandomhouse.com

Most Sentinel books are available at a discount when purchased in
quantity for sales promotions or corporate use. Special editions, which include
personalized covers, excerpts, and corporate imprints, can be created when purchased
in large quantities. For more information, please call (212) 572-2232 or e-mail specialmarkets@
penguinrandomhouse.com. Your local bookstore can also assist with discounted bulk
purchases using the Penguin Random House corporate Business-to-Business program. For
assistance in locating a participating retailer, e-mail B2B@penguinrandomhouse.com.

All Scripture quotations, unless otherwise indicated, are taken from the ESV® Bible
(The Holy Bible, English Standard Version®), copyright © 2001 by Crossway, a publishing
ministry of Good News Publishers. Used by permission. All rights reserved.

Scripture quotations marked (NLT) are taken from the Holy Bible, New Living Translation,
copyright © 1996, 2004, 2015 by Tyndale House Foundation. Used by permission of
Tyndale House Publishers, Carol Stream, Illinois 60188. All rights reserved.

Scripture quotations marked (NASB) are taken from the (NASB®) New American
Standard Bible®, copyright © 1960, 1971, 1977, 1995, 2020 by the Lockman Foundation.
Used by permission. All rights reserved. (www.lockman.org).

Scripture quotations marked (NIV) are taken from the Holy Bible, New International Version®,
NIV®. Copyright © 1973, 1978, 1984, 2011 by Biblica Inc.™ Used by permission of Zondervan. All
rights reserved worldwide. (www.zondervan.com). The "NIV" and "New International Version"
are trademarks registered in the United States Patent and Trademark Office by Biblica Inc.™

Scripture quotations marked (KJV) are taken from the King James Version.

Library of Congress Cataloging-in-Publication Data
Names: Moore, Russell, 1971- author.
Title: Losing our religion : an altar call for evangelical America / Russell Moore.
Description: New York : Sentinel, 2023. | Includes bibliographical references.
Identifiers: LCCN 2023003441 (print) | LCCN 2023003442 (ebook) |
ISBN 9780593541784 (hardcover) | ISBN 9780593541791 (ebook)
Subjects: LCSH: Evangelicalism—United States—History—21st century. |
Church renewal—United States—History—21st century.
Classification: LCC BR526 .M667 2023 (print) | LCC BR526 (ebook) |
DDC 277.308/3—dc23/eng/20230501
LC record available at https://lccn.loc.gov/2023003441
LC ebook record available at https://lccn.loc.gov/2023003442

Printed in the United States of America
1st Printing

BOOK DESIGN BY CHRIS WELCH

To Phillip Bethancourt and Daniel Patterson.

Thank you.

Contents

LOSING
OUR
RELIGION

INTRODUCTION

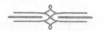

INTRODUCTION

If we wanted to find Jesus, we would have to lose our religion. That's what the preacher said. In fact, he said it every week, every Sunday morning and every Sunday night, and then in the fall and the spring, he would bring in a guest evangelist to tell us the same thing. Religion, he said, gave the wrong answers because it asked the wrong questions. Religion asked, "Am I a church member?" or "Am I an American?" Religion asked, "Am I a moral person?" or "Do my good deeds outweigh my bad?" Religion asked, "Can I assent to the fact that the Bible is true?" or "Can I recite a creed or a catechism?"

Those were the wrong questions, and religion gave the wrong answers. The ultimate questions were deeper, more personal: "Do you know you're a sinner?" and "Do you trust the crucified and risen Jesus to atone for that sin?" and "Will you commit your life to taking up your cross and following him?" For those questions, they would assert, religion would not do, only a relationship, a personal, living faith—not your church's faith, not your country's faith, not your family's faith, but yours. If we were to see the kingdom of God, religion couldn't get us there, they said. We must be born again.

Some people call it an altar call. Some call it a "Come to Jesus" meeting. We called it an "invitation." Though we were low-church Mississippi Baptists, who thought we didn't have any ritual or formality, this was part of our liturgy. Every week, at the end of the service, the gospel would be repeated—about how God so loved the world that he gave his only Son, that whoever believed in him would not perish but have everlasting life. Every week the question "How do I become a Christian?" was answered with step-by-step guidance, sometimes even with a prayer a person could repeat. Every head would be bowed, every eye would be closed, but sometimes we would be looking around, with everybody praying that this would be the week that Miss Velma's husband would go down the aisle, to accept Jesus as his personal Lord and Savior.

Every week was an opportunity, not just for the unbelievers but also for all of us. We would ask ourselves: Is there some sin I need to confess today? Do I need to recommit my life to Christ? Is God calling me to "full-time Christian service," maybe even to be a missionary on the other side of the world? While all these questions—from the pulpit and in our own minds—were being asked, the organ would play quietly in the background hymns we all knew by heart: "Just as I am, without one plea, but that Thy blood was shed for me . . ." or "Softly and tenderly Jesus is calling . . . calling, oh, sinner, come home . . ." or "I have decided to follow Jesus . . . no turning back, no turning back."

When I was older, I found much to criticize about this weekly revivalism. It could communicate a kind of "pray this prayer after me" transaction that propped up the nominal, cultural Christianity all across the Bible Belt. It could substitute the biblical language of justification and sanctification with sentimental phrases about "Asking Jesus into your heart." It could become just as much a formality as could praying the rosary or reciting the Nicene Creed. It could reemphasize the sort of individualized Christianity that enabled generations of my ancestors to fight for the enslavement of human beings or to ignore the atrocities of Jim Crow segregation, all with an easy conscience that all was well as long as they repented of the sins the preacher mentioned—personal sins such as getting drunk or playing cards. It could highlight the emotional manipulation inherent in much American evangelicalism.

But I walked those aisles anyway. I "went forward" to profess my faith in Christ, to pray along with the preacher for God to forgive my sins on the basis of the shed blood of Jesus. I "went forward" to rededicate my life to Christ, after I had grown cynical through a time of doubt. I "went forward" to say that I was "surrendering to preach," that is, to give my life to the calling of ministry to the church. And sometimes I "went forward" just for someone to pray for me, often telling the counselor down front that I had an "unspoken," which we all knew was a prayer request about something one didn't want to talk about at the moment. I knelt at the front of one of those aisles, as the ordained men laid hands on me, setting me apart for ministry.

And I believed it all. I went door-to-door telling people the Good News of the gospel, with a tract showing them how to be born again. Because dancing was considered "worldly," I spent the night of my prom at a Bible study in our church's Family Life Center instead. Drinking wine was considered wrong, so the first alcohol I ever drank was not at a college keg party but at a White House Christmas Party when the server accidentally dipped my cup from the "naughty" bowl instead of the "nice" one. Thanks Obama. Not only did I not lose my virginity until my wedding night, I committed at my ordination to the "Billy Graham rule" of not being alone with a woman not my wife. The altar call not only framed my life; it was my life.

One day, though, the "Come to Jesus" meetings changed. I found myself sitting, sometimes for eight hours at a time, with Southern Baptists like me in heresy trials at which I was not the inquisitor I had been trained to be, but the defendant. I hadn't changed my theology, or my behavior, at all. What I had done, as the president of my denomination's public policy agency, was refuse to endorse Donald Trump.

A denominational leader, after one of the countless "Come to Jesus" meetings at which I was upbraided for sacrificing "unity," articulated with bracing clarity what had been implicit for quite a while. "We can't get rid of you," he said (though they tried). "All our wives and kids are with you, but we can do psychological warfare until you think twice before you open your mouth."

What surprised me was that this vitriol came even from some I had counted as mentors. It was nothing personal, they told me. They just wanted to maintain "influence" with the most rightward fringe of the denomination. Those populists would eventually win, they reasoned, and only those who could "stay at the table" would be able to lead long-term.

A friend, and respected older Baptist leader, called when I was at the lowest moment of all this psychological warfare. I assumed it was to check on me or pray with me. Instead, he acted as though I had betrayed a fraternity into which he had inducted me. "This is not how you play the game," he said. "You give them the 90 percent of the red meat they expect, and then you can do the 10 percent of side stuff that you want to do, on immigrants or whatever." He was right. I had played the game poorly. I didn't consider the culturally conservative positions I took to be "red meat." I was pro-life and pro-family for the same reasons I was pro–racial justice and pro-refugee. I didn't realize that we were playing a game. If so, why would I give thirty years of my life to it? The thought that perhaps that's all this was turned out to be the most effective psychological warfare of all.

The breaking point came, though, when an investigative journalist published a report demonstrating cases of hundreds of people sexually abused and assaulted in Southern Baptist churches, along with multiple allegations of churches having covered up such abuses. In attempting to address accountability for such churches and leaders, we faced stonewalling and retaliation for even the most minimal efforts. We sat in mind-numbing meetings behind closed doors where we heard sexual abuse survivors described as "Potiphar's wife" (the Egyptian ruling figure who made a false accusation of rape against the patriarch Joseph) and other spurious biblical analogies. Survivors were often characterized as "crazy" and, at least by one leader, as possibly worse than the abusers themselves. Alt-Right fundamentalist groups in the denomination implied that the "MeToo movement" within our denomination was a tool of the devil himself, and one of them made the case that those of us saying that racism and misogyny were real problems in our denomination were denying the "sufficiency of Scripture" by embracing "cultural Marxist" movements. That no one questioned how this group was itself not violating the sufficiency of Scripture by making this case via the testimony of avowed atheists, featured in their meetings and resources, was an irony no one seemed to notice. Even fewer seemed to point out that the most revered leaders behind these movements were themselves credibly charged with sexual misconduct.

At a conference I hosted, a national advocate for sexual abuse survivors mentioned publicly, with the woman's permission, the horrific mistreatment a sexual abuse survivor had endured at the hands of a Southern Baptist entity. That entity's president called a meeting to ask me how I could let this happen, and to remind me that I had a responsibility to "protect the base." The problem was not with the sexual abuse crisis itself—we were repeatedly rebuked for using the word *crisis*—but with those who spoke publicly about it. After all, the reasoning went, churches might stop giving to the institutions and that would hurt missionaries, which would hinder the advance of the gospel. All would have been well for me, the message was clear, if I just would treat sexual abuse like an "unspoken" prayer request—a vague and unarticulated concern with no specifics, at least not in public. Within months, that same entity launched (purely coincidentally, they assured me) yet another "investigative task force" to determine whether I and my team were too "liberal."

Through all of it I maintained what some said was a Stockholm syndrome level of loyalty to my Southern Baptist identity. Partly that was because I was convinced that most people in the pews and in the pulpits were unaware of what was happening behind the veil. And I couldn't say anything without those attacking me charging me with being "divisive," and thus prompting my own supporters to ask why I couldn't just give "the brothers" a little bit more of what they wanted, in order not to disrupt the flow of support to our missionaries around the world. And part of it was because I couldn't think of myself as anything other than a Southern Baptist. I was still the kid carrying the Christian flag down the aisle at Vacation Bible School's opening assembly. And when Southern Baptists said, "Depart from me, you worker of iniquity, I never knew you," it sounded to me as if Jesus himself were saying it. So I smiled my way through it all, telling people, when asked, about all the good things Southern Baptists did, and how we couldn't judge them on the basis of a few corrupt people in leadership.

My wife, though, had heard that speech too many times. "I love you. I'm with you to the end. And you can do whatever you want," she said, as we walked out of a particularly hostile Southern Baptist Convention Executive Committee meeting. "But if you're still a Southern Baptist by summer, you'll be in an interfaith marriage." She is not a woman given to ultimatums. But she'd seen and heard too much. By that point, so had I. In that moment, I resolved two things. The first was that I would still trust and obey the Jesus to whom Southern Baptists introduced me, and I would follow him, whether he has a southern accent or not, whether his Jordan River baptism was full immersion or not. And the second was that I would never be at another Baptist business meeting again. I was not losing my faith, but I was losing my religion. The altar call they were issuing had me walking the opposite way, right out the back doors and into a world I'd never known before.

On the other side of that reverse altar call, I started to question everything. Was that all it was? Had it all been a lie? That began a period not just of questioning all my assumptions, but also of simultaneously grieving my lost religious home and my own burdened conscience, recognizing complicity in participating for so long in something that now seemed both inane and predatory. I couldn't help but wonder if the plot twist to the story of American conservative Christianity was that what we thought was the Shire was Mordor all along. I pretend that all of that is past me, but it lingers, in the ringing in my ears of the stress-induced tinnitus that persists to this day, and in the fact that I am still waiting for one sleep without nightmares about the Southern Baptist Convention. But here I am, an accidental exile but an evangelical after all.

My situation was especially public, but it wasn't especially unusual. The issues—political fusion with Trumpism, Christian nationalism, white-identity backlash, the dismissing of issues such as abuse as "social justice" secularism, and several others—are (some of them or all of them) dividing almost every church, almost every family, almost every friendship I know. Every institution—from the presidency to local churches to family dining room tables—seems to be in crisis, almost to the point of breakdown. Where at the beginning of my ministry parents used to seek my counsel about their young-adult children walking away from the faith, I was now more likely to hear from committed younger Christians wondering how to connect with parents who were politically radicalized by conspiracy theories. I was less likely to hear about wayward children going out into "the real world" and losing their faith as I was to hear about wayward parents retreating into an imaginary world and losing their minds. After a near-decade of American evangelical Christianity defined almost wholly in the public view with Trumpism or racism or the predatory sexual or financial or psychological power dynamics of countless leaders, the outside world didn't seem to be judging us by "secular" standards as by our own. Weighed in those balances, we were found wanting. Our kingdom was divided and couldn't stand. Our houses were built upon the sand. The very populist and entrepreneurial energies that led American evangelical Christianity to grow into a world-influencing movement and into a powerful political influence bloc seemed to be what was now undoing us, right down to friendships of decades.

Maybe the problem was the altar calls. Some of our worst impulses could be found there: the revivalist penchant for emotionalism, individualism, novelty, market-driven entrepreneurialism, and a populist energy easily manipulated by the ambitious.

One outside perspective concluded: "A religion that is responsive to the pressures of the market will end up profoundly fractured, with each denomination finding most hateful to God the sins that least tempt its members, while those sins that are the most popular become redefined and even sanctified. In the end, a market-driven approach to religion gives rise to a market-driven approach to truth, and this development ultimately eviscerated conservative Christianity in the U.S. and left it the possession of hypocrites and hucksters."* There was, and is, enough truth in this to sting.

Could such emotional appeals to immediate action unwittingly create a willingness to listen to demagogues who prey on the more primal parts of the human psyche? Could the emphasis on salvation as a critical moment of decision be related to an evangelical need for a clear separation of the sheep and the goats, boundaries

---

*Editorial, "American Christianity: Change and Decay," *The Guardian*, January 15, 2017.

that are much easier to see with a Make America Great Again yard sign than with the invisible moving of the Spirit? Maybe. Judgment of the effectiveness of the preacher's sermon and the skill of the musicians' performance was often based on how many came forward at the end of the service that week. The altar call could give a verifiable sign of success, which is why traveling evangelists always referenced during the "love offering" to fund their ministries how many people had walked the aisle at their last meeting. Could there be a connection between this sort of clamoring for a visible demonstration of our "influence" and the kind that wants to define white evangelicals as leading a "moral majority" or representing the "Real America" beleaguered by coastal elites? Perhaps. Is that connected to the kind of market-driven ethos that has led to an evangelical Christianity determined to be as angry as the people in the pews? Maybe. Is the sort of individualism ("Jesus died for *you*") of such appeals part of what could enable white evangelicals to be the statistically least likely people in America to agree that social justice is an important priority? Likely so. Could the "cheap grace" (walk this aisle and pray this prayer) so easily marketed in our altar calls have been the very thing that enabled Christians to excuse as "locker room talk" a politician boasting of sexual assault or to shield predatory church leaders from accountability for their sins and crimes That's more than a possibility.

And yet.

There's no way to reform the "evangelical church," because there's no such thing as "the Evangelical Church." That's part of the difficulty of this conversation. *Evangelical* is just a word we impose artificially to describe a particular type of Christian. No one signs up at a central office to be an "evangelical." And, in fact, most evangelicals don't ever, to use the language of the moment, "identify" as evangelicals. They might use words like *saved* or *born again* or *Bible-believing Christian.* This fuzzy term is an attempt to categorize a chaotic and contradictory cast of characters, who often have little in common except for a few emphases and aspirations.

Some would suggest that none of the disorienting revelations of the past several years are in any way a "betrayal" of anything within evangelicalism; they are what (at least white) evangelicalism is and always has been. Evangelicalism, they would argue, is not a theological identity, but a cultural one, one built from the beginning on nationalism, racism, militarism, misogyny, populism, or right-wing politics. To some degree, this critique is true. Most people are shaped by cultures and subcultures, not by theological abstractions. One cannot understand the Reformation-era revolt against the system of indulgences if one doesn't understand why anybody would be motivated to buy them. To get that, one would have to know what it is like to believe that one's loved ones might be suffering in purgatory, counting on the prayers of relatives and the intercession of the saints, in order to make the pilgrimage to heaven. Does that settle the question of whether purgatory exists? No. Does it exclude the cultural realities of sixteenth-century Europe that would make that belief credible? No. Does it rule out psychological impulses that might make anxiety about one's eternal state more pronounced? No. The reality is complicated—a theology shaped by a culture and a culture shaped by a theology.

Evangelicalism is much more than a set of theological abstractions. So is Christianity itself, and the atrocities and banalities done in the name of Christianity are multitudinous. Are we unable to find any common strands in what we call "Christianity" as opposed to "Buddhism" or "atheism"? The creeds and confessions do not tell the whole Christian story, but can that story be told without them? As one scholar of religion put it, when one sees even the most unsophisticated spray-painting of Jesus Saves on a fence post, one still must ask, "Who's Jesus?" "Saved from what?" "Why do I need saving?" "Why can't I save myself?"*

If evangelicalism is, and has always been, merely American nationalism or market-driven populism or southern honor culture, then evangelicalism isn't really the problem. What matters, then, is merely the underlying nationalism or populism or honor culture; the beliefs and practices are just a veneer on those things. Even those who would say that evangelicals are *really* about those things would not conclude that the evangelicals themselves think so—as though they were a conspiracy, writing prayers and hymns and holding crusades and starting church-planting movements to cover their real objectives. Even if "the gospel" and "the mission" in evangelical circles were the equivalent of snake oil, one would still be

---

*Hugh Heclo, "Reconsidering Christianity and American Democracy," in *Christianity and American Democracy* (Cambridge: Harvard University Press, 2007), 220.

left with the question: why do people want snake oil? What are the promises the snake-oil salesmen are making, and what do the people buying it expect it to do for them? Is there a difference between the sort of nationalism that says that America should exclude immigrants or dominate the world and the kind that would say all those things are true because God said so? When we talk about sexual harassment or abuse, are we simply talking about what happens in Hollywood or Silicon Valley, or is there, in addition to all of those horrors, another kind of horror in abusing spiritual authority to do those things—telling victims, for instance, that they must stay with abusive husbands in order to "win them to Christ" or that they must "forgive" and "show grace" to the abuser by leaving him unaccountable? What sort of twisted power does the abusing church have when they say that the blood of Christ has covered the transgression, so it should be covered up?

If "evangelicalism" is *just* political idolatry or populist demagoguery or white nationalism or toxic masculinity or something else, then we can get at the problem merely by addressing all of those. What we must face, though, is the fact that as awful as all of those horrors are, they are made *worse* when they are framed as badges of religious identity. Almost every dictator or demagogue has seen this. With religion, one cannot only claim rapacious power but can do it with the unquestionable authority of the divine. "Support us or you are out of the tribe" is a real threat—one that psychological research now shows us is analogous with physical pain. How much worse is all that, plus, "Support us or you just might not be right with God"? A religious authority can make "Support us or to hell with you" feel shockingly literal. Abuse of power is always horrific; how much worse, though, when the abuse comes by a weaponized spiritual authority.

And behind that is the biggest question of all. What if it's true? After all, as Walker Percy once said of a disgraced Pentecostal evangelist of his time: "Just because Jimmy Swaggart believes in God doesn't mean that God does not exist."* What if it's true that unless a person is born again he cannot inherit the kingdom of God? If so, then what's happened to evangelical Christianity is not just a sociological or political crisis, but a spiritual crisis too.

And that's what brings me back to those altar calls.

A generation ago, a historian pondered the question of why evangelical churches were growing while mainline Protestant churches were hemorrhaging members. He explored the possibility—offered by some sociologists and church-growth experts—that "conservative" churches expected more of people (in terms of both belief and behavior), and thus had more "buy-in." And he studied the idea that conservative churches were more attractive to people because they provide a kind of certainty that human beings need. "Thus saith the Lord" is just more definitive than "The Episcopal Church welcomes you." Johnny Cash could record a song called "The Preacher Said 'Jesus Said,'" with recordings of Billy Graham sermons interspersed

---

*Walker Percy, *Signposts in a Strange Land*, ed. Patrick Samway (New York: Farrar, Straus and Giroux, 1991), 159.

throughout that wouldn't have worked as well titled "The Theologian Said 'The Ground of Being,'" with Paul Tillich lectures. And
yet, the historian suggested, these factors, important as they might
be, were not as critical to evangelical success as the fact that evangelicals knew how to create the right kind of crisis. There's a human
longing, he wrote, to start over again—to die to an old self, to cross
a threshold to a new life.* Human beings have a need for rites of
passage, for rites of initiation, and not just those that are slow and
organic but those that are definitive and decisive too. What if, he
wondered, this longing for a certain sort of crisis was created by
God as a way for human beings to, as the apostle Paul put it, "seek
God, and perhaps feel their way toward him and find him" (Acts
17:27)?

Whether expressed in a literal or just in metaphorical altar calls,
the sense of the personal is at the heart of the experience summed
up in what we call "evangelical." And, in that sense, the altar call
represents not just the worst but also the best of evangelical Christianity in America. The emphasis on the personal in evangelical
Christianity can, and has, gone too far, into an individualism that
erodes the visible, palpable nature of the church. We are, after all,
the people who engineered individually packaged plastic communion cups of grape juice, with wafers affixed under a seal on the top.
Because of the Tower of Babel and the atom bomb, I can't say this

---

*Martin Marty, "'Baptistification' Takes Over," *Christianity Today*, September 2,
1983, 34–35.

was the worst human invention of all time, but it took a minute to think about it. Even so, just because an emphasis can be overdone in ways that obscure other essential truths is no sign that the emphasis itself is untrue or unneeded. And maybe now much more than we think. I was wrong to be exasperated hearing my fellow evangelical preachers say that the gospel is "not a religion but a relationship." Yes, the Bible speaks of Christianity as a religion (James 1:27), and it's a perfectly good word. On that I haven't changed my mind. But I wasn't paying enough attention to what those preachers *meant* by religion—namely, a cold, lifeless dogma or a tribal belonging or a moralism directed at earning favor from God.

What if, when I am addressed as a sinner, this is not just a generic category of fallen human nature but is directed at *me*—for *my* sins, no matter how I spin or justify them. What if there really is a Judgment Day, and what if on that day I am not hidden in a nation-state or a family tree or a political tribe or a religious institution? What if I stand there alone, as a person, to account for *my* sins? The metaphorical walk down the aisle, then, is not an ideology and it is not, first, about group belonging. One acknowledges not only that "God loves the world" or that "Christ died for humanity," but "Jesus loves *me*; Jesus died for *me*." Evangelicalism is not meant to be in crisis; evangelicalism is meant to *be* a crisis. That's what being born again is to the person, what revival is to the church. And that means asking—just like those old gospel appeals did—what we have to find and what we have to lose.

One evangelical convert to more liturgical forms of Christianity famously said, "Evangelical is not enough."* He was right. Left to itself, evangelical revivalism is unbalanced, disconnected from the regularity and rhythms of liturgy and from the deeper history of the church. That's why we need the rest of the church. But what evangelical Christianity does offer is needed too—a sense that any given Sunday could result in even the most far-gone sinner radically turned around, finding the carpet on that church aisle or the sawdust on the tent floor to be a Road to Damascus. One respected evangelical biblical scholar attempted to define what an "evangelical" is this way: "An evangelical is one who believes in the God who justifies the ungodly."† Each of those words requires an entire chapter of the book of Romans to unpack. But, as definitions go, it's not a bad start. And that's what, at least in North America, we are in danger of losing.

After the disruptions of the past few years, though, the primary critique of evangelical Christianity—from the outside world as well as from those of us who've found ourselves accidental exiles within the church—is not that evangelical Christianity believes and practices all these things, but that we don't.

Maybe you are one of those people in just such a dark night. Perhaps you look around at the rest of the Christian culture and

---

*Howard Thomas, *Evangelical Is Not Enough: Worship of God in Liturgy and Sacrament*, (Nashville: Nelson, 1988).

†Fleming Rutledge, *The Crucifixion: Understanding the Death of Jesus Christ* (Grand Rapids: Eerdmans, 2015), 575, n. 6.

wonder if you're the crazy one. Maybe you hope that this book is a roadmap to a better evangelical future. It is not. As a matter of fact, our frantic desire to find something—a movement, a curriculum, a funding strategy, whatever—to "fix this" is a key aspect of the kind of "worldliness" that has led us to a church so identified with Machiavelli-like cruelty and Caligula-like vulgarity. If the church is just a human community to be managed, or a technology to be re-programmed, then we should indeed walk away from it because there are better alternatives elsewhere. In another context, the poet and novelist Wendell Berry told a group of activists concerned, as was he, about environmental catastrophe that the worst obstacle to their effort was the idea that the solutions should be as large-scale as the problem. Instead, he noted, "the great problems call for many small solutions." That must start with honesty to name things as they are, and the imagination to see that it doesn't have to be this way. That's frustrating, he acknowledged: "Some will find it an insult to their sense of proportion, others to their sense of drama."[*]

Evangelical Christianity, at its best, is all about "small solutions." Genuine renewal in the church comes, one by one, soul by soul; the temple is built stone by stone. This book is a word of testimony—testimony of what one fellow wayfarer has learned about how to survive when the evangel and the evangelicalism seem to be saying two different things. That requires naming what we have lost—our

---

[*]Wendell Berry, "The Way of Ignorance," in *The World-Ending Fire: The Essential Wendell Berry*, ed. Paul Kingsnorth (London: Penguin, 2017), 334.

credibility, our authority, our identity, our integrity, our stability, and, in many cases, our sanity. This book will consider all the ways evangelical America has sought these things in the wrong way—and suggests that perhaps it's by losing our "life" that we will find it again. Along the way, I will suggest little choices you can make, not just to survive this dispiriting time, but in order to envision a different future.

In 2020, archaeologists unearthed what they believed to be the remains of a fourth-century Byzantine Christian church, built on what was thought to be the place called Caesarea Philippi where the Gospels tell us Jesus once brought his disciples. There he asked them, "Who do people say that the Son of Man is?" The Gospels report that the disciples responded with all the most popular answers among the population: John the Baptist, a returning prophet such as Elijah or Jeremiah of old, and so forth. Only Simon Peter was willing to confess what must have seemed ridiculous if not blasphemous to some who overheard: "You are the Christ, the Son of the living God" (Matt. 16:13–16). Jesus, of course, responded with words both debated and cherished by Christians ever since: "Blessed are you, Simon Bar-Jonah! For flesh and blood has not revealed this to you, but my Father who is in heaven. And I tell you, you are Peter, and upon this rock I will build my church, and the gates of hell shall not prevail against it" (Matt. 16:17–18). What's important about this account is not just *what* happened but *where* it happened.

As the dig showed, the church built to honor the "Upon this

rock" pronouncement wasn't the first house of worship to exist there, but was built on the ruins of another, a temple to the god Pan. As one scholar explained, the spot was a place of worship for Pan since the third century BC, with a temple built there somewhere around 20 BC. If you don't know who Pan is, think of the image that comes to mind when you think of how our culture pictures the devil or, more innocently, of Mister Tumnus from *The Lion, the Witch, and the Wardrobe.* Pan was a satyr god—a goat-like deity devoted to shepherds, music, and raucous sex. This is the sort of place Jesus took his followers, to reveal to them one of the most important aspects of the mystery of his identity and mission. Not only was this a place probably devoted to the most literal pagan forms of nature-worship, but it also was a place that, even earlier, was probably a focus of Canaanite Baal worship.

Moreover, this is the place we most often think of by the name Caesarea Philippi. This is because the area belonged to the house of Herod, whose son Philip named it after himself and the Roman emperor. The place represents both the forces of paganism and the political forces that literally crucified Jesus. The crosses that lined the roads of Rome communicated two things: I can hurt you and I cannot be hurt. Crucifixion didn't just kill; it killed in the most humiliating way possible. In crucifixion, it is impossible to maintain the honor and dignity of a stoic facing quick execution. A crucified person would have his defeat by Rome made awfully public, his nakedness on display as gawkers watched him gasp for breath and scream in agony. The cross was the losing side of a culture war. That threat of crucifixion was there hanging over that monument to political and cultural strength.

What's striking to me in this account is not just that Jesus opposes both the way of Pan and the way of Caesar, but that he does so in a way that is not frantic or frenzied. He has the tranquility that comes from the confidence that his church will be built and that nothing—not even the gates of hell—could overturn that promise. When one feels as though one is under constant existential threat, one cannot maintain the bonds of trust in others needed to build community or the kind of curiosity that can lead to finding ways to serve one another. Confidence in the kingdom of Christ, trust that our ultimate survival is assured in Christ, can enable us then not just to serve our Lord but to stop looking for substitutes for him. Some are panicked about rising secularism and what they fear will be hostility to the church, but act in ways that tie the witness of the church to forms of power that actually fuel secularization. Some of you are tempted toward cynicism, then, when you see people you thought you knew taking positions you never could imagine them taking, because of politics or culture. The first group sometimes speaks as though the church will collapse if "the culture" collapses. And members of the second group sometimes think that the church will not survive the scandals of what passes for Christian "influence" at the moment. Wherever you fit in this spectrum, though, we should all heed exactly what happened at Caesarea Philippi. Jesus rebuked Peter for seeking to adopt the way of Herod and of Caesar and of Baal—power apart from the cross. In fact, Jesus said this was Satan (Matt. 16:23). What Jesus builds is different altogether—a church that cannot be bought with Caesar's coin and cannot be stopped with Caesar's cross.

That promise is not to build "the evangelical movement," whatever that is. It's not a promise that institutions will continue to exist as they are, any more than "For God so loved the world" means that a person can enter the kingdom without taking up the cross. Any church can lose its lampstand, Jesus told us, and flicker out. We are more vulnerable than we know. Even so, there is still power in the blood. Maybe, like the old altar calls, this is a moment of decision—decisions about what to seek and what to flee, what to save and what to lose. Maybe "losing our religion" is just another way of saying what Jesus commanded a first century church in crisis—a rekindling of our first love (Rev. 2:4). If the stories are true—and I believe they are—then maybe we should listen to what they've told us all along. Only when something is lost can it be found. Only when something dies can it be born again.

CHAPTER ONE

LOSING OUR CREDIBILITY

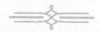

How Disillusion Can Save Us
from Deconstruction

S omething was happening at the Vatican, though I can't remember what it was. Maybe it was another revelation about
sexual abuse cover-up, or maybe it was another contentious
synod meeting. All I know is the feeling I had when I saw a woman
I knew to be a serious Roman Catholic, post, with no commentary,
an old music video on social media. The video, R.E.M.'s "Losing
My Religion," was from 1991—far long enough time for a musical
hit to be unrecognizable to most people under a certain age. This
song is different, though, because of the way it had entered popular culture—as the soundtrack to almost any story about an ex-
Catholic or an "exvangelical" or about someone leaving a New Age
cult or a jihadist cell or any other sort of religious identity. The
song's usage was so common that many wondered if this woman
was announcing that she was losing her faith. She responded to
those questions by assuring people that, no, she had not lost her

faith at all. She was afraid, though, that she was losing her church. It was not that she didn't believe what her church had taught her but that she didn't believe her church believed what her church had taught her.

How this old song could communicate so quickly a loss of personal faith is not difficult to see. To a haunting tune, the lyrics point to both loss and confusion: "That's me in the corner, that's me in the spotlight, losing my religion." The song implies a clamoring to stay within the community ("trying to keep up with you") and the odd mixture of isolation and hypervisibility that comes from not being able to do so (both the corner and the spotlight). With all of that comes the implication of the also uncanny combination of guilt about the disloyalty of speaking up and the guilt about the complicity of staying silent for so long.

What most people don't pick up from the song—maybe because of the deceptively bouncy melody—is that it's not so much about doubt as it is about anger. Those who assume the song to be an attack on institutionalized religion would have credible reasons for assuming so. The songwriter, John Michael Stipe, was from a long line of Methodist ministers and is now a kind of Zen Buddhist of the Californian sort. He wrote his music from Athens, Georgia, a little island of bohemian free-thinking in a surrounding sea of Bible Belt fundamentalism. And yet, at least according to the publication *American Songwriter*, the song is misunderstood. The "losing my religion" referenced here is based on the old southern expression that conveys the moment when "politeness gives way to anger."*

It's less "I don't find the ontological argument for the existence of God believable anymore; I'm losing my religion," and more "If I wait in this Department of Motor Vehicles line for one more minute, I'm going to lose my religion," or, "If she keeps bringing up Uncle Ronnie's ex-wife here at the Thanksgiving table, he's going to lose his religion with her."

As the years have gone by, though, I'm not sure that there's always a hard break between loss of belief and politeness giving way to anger. Perhaps at this moment of history, both interpretations of the song are true. In a time of secularization, maybe many who were once bound to religious communities by habit and communal ties now find that they can't intellectually hold on to religion anymore. But maybe the primary problem right now is not about intellect and argumentation, but about grief, betrayal, and even rage at what can be done by religion.

When the events of the last half decade hit, some people wondered if I would grow disillusioned with the church, or with Christ, and maybe even lose my faith. I never did, and when asked why, I can only speculate that it's because this wasn't my first crisis of disillusionment. When I was fifteen years old, I contemplated suicide

---

*Evan Schlansky, "Behind the Song: R.E.M., 'Losing My Religion,'" *American Songwriter*, March 2, 2011.

due to the fear of losing my religion, in both senses of the phrase. As I've written elsewhere, some of it was because of the raw racism around me in the Bible Belt, which I couldn't reconcile with the Bible. We were told not to "conform to the pattern of this world," except, it seemed, when "the world" was the remnant outposts of the Confederate States of America. Part of it was that, just as a journalist knows what a politician's statement means when it says "Senator Smith has decided to spend more time with his family," I knew what the church meant when it said, "The Lord has called Brother Jones from the pastorate into itinerant evangelism." And in both cases it meant someone, somewhere, had proof of something shady in the bedroom or in a bank account. Part of it was politics. Even as a teenager, I could see that the "voting guides" for candidates who would support "Christian morality" and "traditional family values" all tended to mimic exactly the list of issues emphasized that year by the political party most people in the pews supported. The tactics seemed the same as any other political interest group, except with a bigger celebrity endorsement, that of Jesus of Nazareth. With the politics came apocalyptic warnings that "this is the most important election in our lifetimes," and if these candidates weren't elected, we would "lose our entire culture." But when those candidates lost, no one headed for the bunkers. The culture didn't fall—at least not any more than it had before.

The real issue, though, was none of these matters on its own. Behind all of that was a dread deep within me that Christianity might just be southern culture of politics, with Jesus affixed as a hood ornament. If the gospel was just a way to mobilize voters for party bosses or to fund prostitutes and cocaine for preachers on television, that realization would be more than just an adolescent cynical awakening. It would mean, I thought, that the universe itself was a random, meaningless void in which only the fittest survive, and even then not for long. I knew there was much to love in the southern culture around me, but I could also see that just underneath the surface there was also an undercurrent of violence and hatred and seething passions of all sorts. If the gospel were just a means to propping all that up, then that would mean that these weren't aberrations, but the way the universe is, right down to the core.

My parents had read the Chronicles of Narnia, though, and then I read them over and over again on my own, so as a teenager in terror I returned to C. S. Lewis, and read everything he wrote that I could find. What made the difference for me were not his arguments. My problems weren't primarily intellectual. What made the difference for me was the tone of voice I could almost hear in his writing. He was not trying to mobilize me or market to me, and I was able to follow that voice right through the wardrobe and into the broader streams of the broader church that spans heaven and earth, time and eternity, awesome as an army with banners. The crisis was terrible, and the crucible of it is never too far from the surface of my psyche, but I'm glad it happened. It was a manageable crisis that taught me how to tell the difference between the glories of Christ and the terrors that could be the church. But what, I wonder, would have happened to fifteen-year-old Russell Moore if that crisis had happened not in the 1980s but in the 2020s? Would I have ended up the sort of atheist or agnostic or deconstructing exvangelical that I find myself counseling almost every day now? Or, worse, would someone have found me hanging from a rope, with my King James Bible just beyond the reach of my cold dead hands? Who can know? I suppose I should just conclude, with apologies to Paul Simon, that I was born again at the right time.

But what about you? The context in which you are making your decisions is strikingly different, and so are the stakes.

In 2021, a Gallup survey of American religious affiliations and habits showed that the number of Americans now affiliated with a church or other house of worship is just 47 percent. Even more significant than this low number is the dizzying speed of the plummet—from around 68 percent of Americans twenty years ago. And the numbers are even starker than they appear. Generation X is less affiliated than Baby Boomers. Millennials are less affiliated than Generation X, and Generation Z will be the least affiliated of them all. What's more, the most reliable studies show us that as little as 8 percent of white Millennials identify as "evangelical Christian," as compared with 26 percent of senior adults. Again, the numbers for the youngest generations are even more jarring—with 34 percent identifying as religiously unaffiliated, and that number is growing.* Another major study forecast that fewer than half of Americans would be Christian by 2070, even using several projected models, including one in which current rates of affiliation and disaffiliation remain stable and another in which there is continued growth in disaffiliation.†

Referring to the "Nones," those claiming "no religious affiliation," sociologist Philip Jenkins contends: "America's religious future appears to be None."‡ Jenkins argues that statistics on the age of people in congregations presents a dire situation for the churches of the next generation. He writes. "By mid-century, the heart-rending politics of church closures due to congregations 'aging out' will be a critical and deeply divisive theme in denominational affairs." The reasons for the rise of the Nones are complicated, to be sure, but Jenkins says we can see the general patterns. "When a 2018 study asked 'nothing in particulars' why they rejected religious affiliation, 47 percent disliked the positions churches took on social or political issues, and 31 percent disliked religious leaders," Jenkins notes. "Only 21 percent denied a belief in God. I suspect that as

---

*"The Politicization of White Evangelical Christianity Is Hurting It," *The Economist,* February 28, 2019, cited in Tara Isabella Burton, *Strange Rites: New Religions for a Godless World* (New York: PublicAffairs, 2020), 239.

†Bob Smietana, "Fewer Than Half of Americans Will Be Christian by 2070, According to New Projections," *Christian Century,* November 2022, 20–21.

‡Phillip Jenkins, *Fertility and Faith: The Demographic Revolution and the Transformation of World Religions* (Waco: Baylor University Press, 2020), 104.

future surveys track the numbers of Nones, we will see a steep up-swing during and following that traumatic election year of 2016. How could we not?"* Jenkins names several factors to why Nones are repelled from identifying with generic labels such as evangelical. These include a sense that *evangelical* is "a synonym for Republican causes of the most reactionary kind," an intuition that such political activism is "a thin disguise for white racial self- interest," and a "general air of scandal" around religious institutions accelerating after the revelations of the Roman Catholic sexual abuse scandals.† As far back as 2010, political scientists Robert Putnam and David Campbell looked at the growth patterns of American religions and noted that "the evangelical boom that began in the 1970s was over by the early 1990s, nearly two decades ago." They concluded, "In twenty-first century America expansive evangelicalism is a feature of the past, not the present."‡

In terms of numbers, the death of evangelical Christianity is exaggerated. At the same time that mainline Protestant and Roman Catholic memberships have plummeted, the total number of evangelical Christians has remained relatively steady, but the disaffiliation rates are startling. Some of the disaffiliation, to be sure, is due to liberalizing cultural norms, decreasing fertility, and increasing

---

*Ibid., 106–7.

†Ibid.

‡Robert D. Putnam and David E. Campbell, *American Grace: How Religion Divides and Unites Us* (New York: Simon & Schuster, 2010), 105.

mobility. But the evidence is mounting that a significant amount of secularization is accelerated and driven not by the "secular culture" but by evangelicalism itself. Many have pointed to compelling data—from Putnam and Campbell and other sociologists and political scientists and demographers—showing that the politicization of American religion is a key driver of people away from religious affiliation. Some would point to the fact that most of those leaving would identify politically as somewhere from moderate to progressive, to suggest that such people are better off outside the church in the first place. Let's just assume for the sake of argument that such is true, which comes first here—the demand to line up politically in order to follow Jesus or the decision to reject the politics of those making such demands? If Christianity is politics, people can get their politics from somewhere else—and fight and fornicate and get drunk too—all without giving up a Sunday morning. And, in fact, many are doing just that—not only among those who are leaving but among those who are "staying" too.

Political scientist Daniel K. Williams writes, "If 'lapsed evangelical Protestant' were a denomination, it would be by far the largest religious body in the South." Again contrary to the myths of progressive secularization, Williams mines the data to show that these de-churched "evangelicals" are not becoming like Swedes, or even like de-churched northeastern cradle Catholics. Their politics haven't changed (except by becoming more extreme) and their sense of religious identity hasn't changed either. The data show that they are liberalizing, to be sure, but only on the specific sins they want to commit—especially when it comes to premarital sex. "When people leave church, they retain the moralism—at least insofar as it pertains to other people—but lose the sense of self-sacrifice and trust in others," Williams writes. "They keep their Bible, their gun, their pro-life pin, and their MAGA hat, but also pick up a condom and a marijuana joint and lose whatever willingness they had to care for other people in community."*

Some progressive secularists assumed that secularization equals "progress" (liberally defined) and that, essentially, people who stopped going to church would replace it with mimosa brunches discussing the topics on National Public Radio. Instead, the near reverse is happening—culture wars without worship and connection do not end the culture wars; they, in many cases, heighten them. Almost any disconnection of people from organic community leads to extremism and anger—no matter the place on the ideological spectrum. Consider the evolution of the Left, from the days when leadership was wielded mostly by labor unions of plumbers, teamsters, electricians, etc., and civil rights leaders who were, almost to a person, pastors or pillars of local congregations. Studies show that these de-churched Protestants are far more hyper-individualistic, cynical, and distrustful of others, Williams writes, much more likely to say that most people are out to take advantage of others. They are also much more likely to be lonely, disconnected, suspicious of

---

*Daniel K. Williams, "White Southern Evangelicals Are Leaving the Church," *Christianity Today*, August 2, 2022.

institutions, and angry. When the church is raptured from a person's life and all that's left are culture wars, the result is not good for anyone. As one critic of identity politics put it, "An affiliation is not an experience. It is, in fact, a surrogate for experience. Identity is the articulation of this surrogacy. Where the faith in God is wanting, there is still religious identity. Where the bed is cold and empty, there is still sexual identity. Where the words of the fathers are forgotten, there is still ethnic identity. The thinner the identity, the louder."* That's why we are in a time in which crazy is itself a church-growth strategy. Crafty entrepreneurs know that, in the absence of biblical literacy or real Christian grounding, the more extreme and outrageous one becomes, for some people it will sound like "conviction." We can see this pioneered over the past half century by talk radio, both Christian and non-Christian. Talk radio comes with the illusion of authority. The person behind the microphone would seem to be a leader, helping people to know how to think and respond to issues. But it rarely works like that. Instead, talk-radio hosts actually don't tell their audiences what to be angry about. They figure out what their audiences—or at least potential callers—are *already* angry about, and then channel outrage for them. A lewd shock jock could decide that sexual libertinism and misogyny were bad—and his base would be asking, "What happened to you?" A conservative talk-show host could say that he's persuaded that climate change is real—and his audience would not thereby become curious about renewable

---

*Leon Wieseltier, *Against Identity* (New York: William Drentzel, 1996), 10.

energy. The easiest way to success is to erase nuance, to seem to be leading the crowds while actually following them. The same is now happening in churches that become seeker-sensitive worship services, except for angry people and conspiracy theorists. Crazy wins—in the short run. To gain attention, spectacle is the way to be noticed, which is why ambitious but hollow young men on social media often are looking to be denounced, so that they can gain a niche audience. No one will book a congressman on cable television for negotiating a compromise on an infrastructure bill, but everyone will talk to the politician who says that Jewish space lasers are causing wildfires. And one can certainly raise wheelbarrows full of cash by saying extreme things in extreme ways. Television evangelists have known this for years. When this kind of craziness becomes a church growth strategy, we abandon speaking to a mission field with, as the apostle Peter put it, "a reason for the hope that is in you" (1 Pet. 3:15) and embrace instead the goal of a kind of cave of Adullam for "everyone who was in distress, and everyone who was in debt, and everyone who was bitter in soul" to be gathered together (1 Sam. 22:2). The people who leave the "ordinary" worship of Word and discipleship to find places that "tell it like it is" often define that as whoever can provoke the most outrage. The gospel is a sign of contradiction, not a sign of insanity. The gospel is "foolishness" to the world (1 Cor. 1:27), the apostle Paul wrote, but then wrote in the exact same letter that when outsiders are convinced we are out of our minds because of our own incoherence, that's our problem, not theirs (1 Cor. 14:23).

And we end up with the kind of confusing cultural mix in which

Nones think they are evangelicals, and evangelicals worry they are Nones. What seems different about this quiet exodus is that the departures are heightened not among the peripheries of the church—those "nominal" or "cultural" Christians who grow up to rebel against their parents' beliefs—but instead among those who are the *most* committed to what were previously thought to be the *hardest* aspects of Christian religion in modernity: belief in "the supernatural," the rigorous demands of discipleship, and a longing for community and accountability in a multigenerational church with ancient roots and transcendent authority. Where a de-churched (to use an anachronistic term) exvangelical (to use another) in the early 1920s was likely to have walked away due to the fact that she found the virgin birth or the bodily resurrection to be outdated and superstitious or because he found moral libertinism to be more attractive than the "outmoded" strict moral code of his past or because she wanted to escape the stifling bonds of a home church for an autonomous individualism, now we see a markedly different—and jarring—model of a disillusioned evangelical. We see now young evangelicals walking away from evangelicalism not because they do not believe what the church teaches, but because they believe the *church itself* does not believe what the church teaches. And, more than that, many have concluded that the church itself is a moral problem.

Again, some of this is hardly new. Martin Luther was partially "radicalized" prior to the Protestant Reformation by seeing the immorality and corruption of priests. *Elmer Gantry* was not only a bestselling novel, it also turned the name into an enduring label for a certain kind of manipulative and shady preacher, precisely because people had, and have, a category for such a thing. In the 1980s, US bankruptcy judge Rufus Reynolds was assigned the case of television evangelists Jim and Tammy Bakker, who fleeced their electronic flock financially, even apart from the sex scandal that came to light at roughly the same time. A woman called the court to ask whether the judge was a Christian. He said, "You tell her I was when I started this case, but now I plead the Fifth Amendment."* Every generation has had to articulate the standard trope that one should not "judge the church by the hypocrites in it," along with the reiteration that even Christian leaders are sinners and susceptible to the weakness of the flesh. At the moment, though, one can hardly blame the cynicism coming toward the church on an overly idealized view of the church or of human nature.

In a study of Catholic disaffiliation in the United Kingdom and North America, sociologist Stephen Bullivant found the scandals to loom large in reasons that people were giving up on the church altogether. This was not simply based on the anger and betrayal that people feel by such atrocities and their cover-ups, although that's certainly the case. It's also the case, though, that this abusive and predatory behavior destroys the very things necessary for any religious community: the belonging that comes from membership

---

*John Wigger, *PTL: The Rise and Fall of Jim and Tammy Bakker's Evangelical Empire* (New York: Oxford University Press, 2017), 295.

---

in a community one can trust.* The scandals and sexual-abuse cover-ups reveal a church that operates with the exact same forms of power maintenance and institutional self-protection as the worst of other institutions with which they are already disillusioned. The church, they find, is just like all the rest. Cultures have been here before. Jacques Barzun argues that the widespread denunciation of "moral turpitude" in the church in the lead-up to the Reformation was about more than hypocrisy; it was about meaning. "The priest, instead of being a teacher, was ignorant; the monk, instead of helping to save the world by his piety, was an idle profiteer; the bishop, instead of supervising the care of souls in his diocese was a politician and businessman." The sheer immovability of all this revealed the situation to be not just declining but decadent. "When people accept futility and the absurd as normal; the culture is decadent," he writes. "The term is not a slur; it is a technical label."† The fact that so many—both those leaving and those staying—are giving up on the situation ever changing is a sign that we in American Christian life have started to accept futility and the absurd as normal.

We might reassure ourselves when we see the proliferating Nones among our youth that the reason they are leaving is because they

---

*Stephen Bullivant, *Mass Exodus: Catholic Disaffiliation in Britain and America Since World War II* (New York: Oxford University Press, 2019), 8–9.

†Jacques Barzun, *From Dawn to Decadence, 1500 to the Present: 500 Years of Western Cultural Life* (New York: HarperCollins, 2000), 11.

want to run their own lives and pursue the sexual hedonism the church (rightly) forbids. Some of that is no doubt the case. But if one believes the Bible, one knows that wanting to run one's own life is not a new development with modernity. And one need only know a little bit of high school biology to know that the desire for sexual hedonism didn't start during the Obama administration. First-century Athens, Greece, was just as intellectually averse to Christianity as is twenty-first-century Athens, Georgia—and far more sexually "liberated" too. And the gospel went forth and the churches grew. The problem now is not that people think the church's way of life is too demanding, too morally rigorous, but that they have come to think the church doesn't believe its own moral teachings.

The problem is not that they reject the idea that God could send anyone to hell but that, when they see the church covering up predatory behavior in its institutions, they have evidence that the church believes God would not send "our kind of people" to hell. If people reject the church because they reject Jesus and the gospel, we should be saddened but not surprised. But what happens when people reject the church because they think *we* reject Jesus and the gospel? If people leave the church because they want to gratify the flesh with abandon, such has always been the case, but what happens when people leave because they believe *the church* exists to gratify the flesh—whether in orgies of sex or orgies of anger or orgies of materialism? That's a far different problem. And what if people don't leave the church because they disapprove of Jesus, but because they've read the Bible and have come to the conclusion that the church itself would disapprove of Jesus? That's a catastrophe.

Bullivant names this catastrophe, as he distinguishes between secularization—as we've known it in the past—and these disillusioned ex- or almost ex-Christians. He argues that they are not, in fact, Nones, a category that, by definition, refers to people with "no religious affiliation." Someone who was reared in a home with "free-thinker" secularist parents might well grow up to embrace the values they were taught. That person would be a None. What we are referring to, though, with a loss of faith in those reared in Christian homes and churches, he refers to as "Nonverts." The difference in this categorization is that a person is "not married" to billions and billions of people. The difference between a None and a Nonvert is the difference between a person's posture toward those billions of people to which he or she is not married and the posture of someone toward an ex-spouse.* Now some people have a perfectly civil relationship with an ex-spouse after a divorce. Maybe they spend holidays together with their children. I've even heard of situations where a couple divorce but still live in the same home. In many other situations, a person grieves the loss of the spouse by divorce as one would grieve the loss of a spouse through death. And in still other situations, a person burns with rage toward the person from whom they split. Whatever the circumstance, though, there is

---

*Stephen Bullivant, *Nonverts: The Making of Ex-Christian America* (New York: Oxford University Press, 2022).

a difference, for everybody, between the ex-spouse and the non-spouse. As the saying goes, one can stop believing, but one cannot stop having been a believer. That has massive implications for society, for churches, and for the spiritual and mental health of countless people.

This crisis of credibility is not just about, or even primarily about, the potential for numbers walking away from the church. The danger might be even greater for those who stay than for those who leave. After all, there's more than one way to "deconstruct" a faith. The most dangerous forms of deconstruction are not those experienced by people who are doubting or scandalized or traumatized by what they've seen and experienced in the church. Some might have concluded that John the Baptist was "deconstructing" when he sent his disciples to ask Jesus, "Are you the one who is to come, or shall we look for another?" (Luke 7:20). The question is not whether we will deconstruct, but *what* we will deconstruct. Will it be the wood, hay, and stubble that is destined to burn up and burn out? Or will it be our own souls? Sometimes those we think are deconstructing are just grieving and asking, as many have before them, where God is in a moment like this. Some who are confident and certain—and scanning the horizon for heretics—are, in fact, those who have given up on the possibility of the new birth, on the renewal of the mind, on the reality of the Judgment Seat of Christ. All that is left, then, is a pseudo-orthodoxy detached from a living faith into a cultivated brand. Following this way means that one has deconstructed not into skepticism but into cynicism. Once the institution is all that's left—or "the movement" or "the cause" or "the theology" or, even worse, one's own position and platform, one has torn down in oneself the very character needed to protect and build those institutions and, even worse than that, one has deadened the sort of conscience needed to hear the call to repent. One may be a hack easily enough in the marketplace or in the political arena, greatly harming one's soul, but year after year of playing to whatever "the base" wants or expects from the church of Jesus Christ does something not just to the institution, and not just to the lives of those harmed by the institution, but also to the souls of those playing the game. Once you have whittled down your moral principles to those that are useful in maintaining your place of belonging, you have, in fact, deconstructed, but not in any positive sense of that term. You have deconstructed not your beliefs but yourself. You have lost not your religion but your soul.

So what's at stake for the church?

Not many Christians have passages from the books of 1 or 2 Kings stitched and hanging in decorative frames on their walls. These books are dark, even by Old Testament history standards. But perhaps we should pay attention to a strange incident in 2 Kings 20, having to do with King Hezekiah, an incident so apparently important that it is repeated almost verbatim later in Isaiah chapter 39. Hezekiah—one of the few admirable kings described in the books of Kings and Chronicles—was healed of a disease and granted fifteen more years of life. He lived, though, with the backdrop of the existential threat of Assyrian forces eager to conquer and overthrow. Against this backdrop, envoys from Babylon traveled to Hezekiah's throne bearing from the Babylonian royal family letters and a present for Hezekiah, for they had heard of his sickness. "And Hezekiah welcomed them, and he showed them all his treasure house, the silver, the gold, the spices, the precious oil, his armory, all that was found in his storehouses," the Bible recounts. "There was nothing in his house or in all his realm that Hezekiah did not show them" (2 Kings 20:13).

The prophet Isaiah approached the king, to ask what these envoys had seen. "And Hezekiah answered, 'They have seen all that is in my house; there is nothing in my storehouses that I did not show them'" (2 Kings 20:15). Isaiah's response was foreboding, as he relays an oracle from God that everything stored up to that point will one day be carted off to Babylon, and that some of Hezekiah's own sons will be exiles, eunuchs in the palace of the king of Babylon. God's denunciation is not (in this case) of the Babylonians. The problem is not the nations acting as the nations do, but Hezekiah. He displayed before a potential geopolitical ally, and potential geopolitical adversary, his power—expressed in military might and economic wealth. At the moment, his values are their values. This is understandable, as Hezekiah no doubt viewed the moment as a binary choice—the Assyrians or the Babylonians. Hezekiah, though, had seen a different sort of power in the past. He, after all, had been rescued from the valley of the shadow of death by God's mercy. When faced with the taunts of the Assyrians of their might and power, Hezekiah took the letter and "went up to the house of the

LORD and spread it before the LORD" (2 Kings 19:14). Hezekiah had seen how the bronze serpent—previously a sign of Israel's vulnerability (those dying from serpent venom would look to the image of the very thing plaguing them in order to be healed) had been twisted into a totem of power, with the people of Israel making offerings to it (2 Kings 18:4). Just as Hezekiah's forefather had erred in seeking security in a census counting the people of God rather than the promise made to Abraham of a people more numerous than the sands of the shore or the stars of the sky, Hezekiah sought to counter verifiable strength with verifiable strength—as though Israel was just another nation, with just another transactional tribal god who would exchange protection for worship. What's instructive for American evangelicalism at the moment is not only Hezekiah's crisis of integrity, but also his response to the message of coming doom. "'The word of the LORD that you have spoken is good,'" Hezekiah replied to Isaiah. "For he thought, 'Why not, if there will be peace and security in my days?'" (2 Kings 20:19). Hezekiah reassured himself about future judgment because of his present tranquility and safety. He was willing to sacrifice his children's future for his present moment. To sacrifice the future for the sake of the present is a crisis of credibility, a crisis of faith.

You can resolve to do better for future generations, but you are only one person. What can you do to follow Christ in a time when the church seems to be losing credibility at a rapid pace?

Embrace the Disillusionment. To see what I mean let's return to the writer who helped, from the grave, to pull me out of my teenage spiritual crisis: C. S. Lewis. In recommending Lewis to some friends who asked where they should begin, I started pulling random Lewis books from my shelf, to talk about what to expect in each title. When I opened one of them, a collection of essays called *The Weight of Glory*, the cover flipped open and I could see the highlights I'd made in the text and the notes I'd written in the margins. It had been years, maybe decades, since I'd read it. Afterward, I kept *The Weight of Glory* out to see what my notes and markings were. One essay, only one, had no marks or notes of any kind.

That essay was Lewis's "Learning in War-Time," a sermon that he delivered in the Church of St. Mary the Virgin in Oxford in the autumn of 1939. I realized that my younger self, reading *The Weight of Glory*, would have seen immediate relevance in almost all the rest of the volume, but probably saw the "Learning in War-Time" chapter as more of a historical relic than an ongoing concern. After all, Lewis's subject in that sermon was to students at Oxford, in a war-threatened England, about why they should bother to study when their country was under attack and the entire globe was convulsing under the weight of World War II. That seemed to be from a distant time, someone else's concern. It doesn't seem that way now.

In his sermon, Lewis addressed a number of obstacles to focusing the mind in a time of crisis. All of them are relevant, but I want to focus on one here that seems to be of particular concern to many of us, and that is what Lewis calls "frustration." The frustration Lewis talked about was both a sense of limited time, "the feeling that we shall not have time to finish," and a sense of futility—this is going to fail, so why do we give attention to it? That certainly seems relevant to the present moment. Much of what we face leaves us helpless before it, no matter how much motivational talk we give ourselves. And that's where Lewis cheers me with his motivational pessimism. He tells us that we should not be surprised by the helplessness and frustration we feel because, in one sense, *everything* we do comes to nothing.

One could easily conclude, "I am going to die someday, so why would I bother with nutrition and hydration?" or a Christian could say, "I'm still going to be a sinner twenty years from now, if I live that long, so why do I try to pursue holiness now? Let's just find some cocaine and prostitutes." God forbid. What we have is the present, and for that we must give an account. "It is only our *daily* bread that we are encouraged to ask for," he said. "The present is the only time which any duty can be done or any grace received." Knowing that, we can be faithful in the moment, even when we don't know the future, the outcome, our success or failure or even how to gauge those things. That's because, Lewis reminds us, the crises we face are unveilings of awful realities, heightened manifestations of awful things, but they are all preexisting conditions. We don't know what the future holds—for our democracy, for our church. Will the center hold? Will our social and civic norms hold or splinter apart? Those are very real questions, but they are heightened intensifications of what we face every second of our lives. That's why Lewis wrote that "there is no question of death or life for any of us, only a question of this death or of that—of a machine gun bullet now or a cancer forty years later."

That sort of pessimism can lead you to devilish places of cynicism and inaction. "Well, we're all going to die of something, so let's not worry when conspiracy theories keep people from life-saving vaccines," or "Well, hatred goes all the way back to Cain and Abel so let's just ignore our consciences when they show us our part in it." Jesus warns us against this sort of sloughing off of our stewardship (Matt. 25:15–28) and so do his apostles (2 Cor. 5:10; Gal. 6:9; 2 Thess. 3:13). Instead, Lewis argued, that frustration and feeling of helplessness should lead us somewhere else—to the right kind of disillusionment. "All the animal life in us, all schemes of happiness that centered on this world, were always doomed to a final frustration," he said. "In ordinary times only a wise man can realize it. Now the stupidest of us knows. We see unmistakably the sort of universe in which we have all along been living, and must come to terms with it."

How do you come to terms with it? You don't do so by normalizing the rot, nor by denying that it exists, much less by sanctifying it as though it were holy. You allow the realization that something is wrong to quite literally dis-illusion you—to remove the illusions you once had. Only then can you cry out for an alternative, or even start to long for one. The death of your illusions, then, is not meant to paralyze you, but to reshape you into the kind of person who can weep and groan at the wreckage around you, which is the first step, of course, to seeking a different sort of kingdom. Your idols failing you is not bad news for you; that you can *see* that they are failing is, in fact, grace. As Lewis told those students: "If we looked for something that would turn the present world from a place of pilgrimage into a permanent city satisfying the soul of man, we are disillusioned, and not a moment too soon."

Not a moment too soon.

Disillusionment can lead to awful places—to cynicism, to laziness, to inaction, to despair. Or it can lead one to let go of every other stable place, and retrace one's steps to the bush aflame with the weight of glory, a bush that does not tell us why things are the way they are, but tells us only "I Am That Which I Am." Sometimes becoming accidental exiles is itself a grace. It can give us the distance to see what matters, and what doesn't. That's true not only for individuals but also for churches, communities, and movements. And as Søren Kierkegaard wrote in the context of a lifeless but "established" Danish church, the most dangerous illusion of all is a paganism that thinks it is Christian. That illusion, he wrote, must be debunked before the gospel can be heard. The difficulty is that, from the standpoint of the illusion, "it looks indeed as if introducing Christianity amounts to taking Christianity away." Nevertheless, he concluded, "this is precisely what must be done, for the illusion must go."* When our illusions start to fall, and our idols disappoint us, this is a moment not of abandonment but of grace.

Provocations: Spiritual Writings of Kierkegaard, ed. Charles E. Moore (Walden, NY: Plough, 2002), 396.

And what that grace always brings is an initial, and sometimes seemingly interminable, period when one feels disoriented and as though one does not know what to do, or where to go. This is part of the grace. That can lead us away from both denial and despair. When asked how it is that he did not yield to the totalitarian overlords behind the Iron Curtain, the poet Czeslaw Milosz wrote, "Perhaps my life was triumphant not because it lacked evil and defeats but because I could see with my own eyes how what was just a vague promise is slowly being fulfilled and that which I suspected of false greatness is disintegrating." Both of those elements were necessary—the promises to be fulfilled and the false greatness that disintegrates. He concluded: "Nevertheless, almost never, with the exception of a few brief moments, did the conviction abandon me that sooner or later the absurd will fail, and this is what distinguished me from my despairing contemporaries."* This can be true of you too.

Recognize Apocalypse. In explaining how storytelling works, one filmmaker said that there are really only two kinds of end-of-the-world movies: "Stop the Apocalypse" or "Survive the Apocalypse."† The "stop the apocalypse" genre is about some threat—maybe a meteor heading for earth—that is averted by grit, expertise, and self-sacrifice, sometimes with an unexpected plot twist near the end,

---

*Czeslaw Milosz, *To Begin Where I Am: Selected Essays* (New York: Farrar, Straus & Giroux, 2001), 434.

†Derek Thompson, *Hit Makers: How to Succeed in an Age of Distraction* (New York: Penguin, 2018).

averting disaster. The "survive the apocalypse" genre is about an aftermath, about people seeking to hold their lives together after a nuclear winter or a zombie plague or an alien invasion. Within evangelical Christianity, some assume the "stop the apocalypse" stance—thinking that a "battle for the soul of evangelicalism" will vanquish the losers and let the winners start over. Or they might think the answer is a detailed discipleship strategy to shape a new generation of Christians to model a better witness to the world. The "survive the apocalypse" people think we should wait patiently for the tumult of the present cultural moment to pass so that something—a Great Awakening or a theological recovery or a generational transition—will come along to undo all the damage of the past few years will come along. Some of these aspects, no doubt, must be a part of the Christian future, but neither alone seems to fit this moment when, as one scholar notes, we live in a time when the hoofbeats of the biblical Four Horsemen of the Apocalypse—rancor, pestilence want, and fury—have seemed awfully loud over the last decade. "Each exposed weakness and rot in institutions whose integrity Americans had long taken for granted," Andrew Bacevich writes. "Each caught members of the nation's reigning power elite by surprise," and each "fostered a sense of things coming undone."[*]

American evangelical Christianity is deeply connected to the

---

[*]Andrew Bacevich, *After the Apocalypse: America's Role in a World Transformed* (New York: Henry Holt, 2021), 2.

apocalyptic, often in ways that rightly draw the derision of the world around us. We are the people who are quick to announce in the aftermath of any disaster exactly who God was punishing by letting it happen, and we are the ones whose prophecy charts have predicted the imminent end of the world time and time again, always, so far, wrongly. If you see someone on a street corner yelling "judgment is coming!," that's likely not a Unitarian; he's one of ours. And yet, despite all of that, the evangelical emphasis on apocalypse as crisis gets at something resonant, in both the biblical text and the human experience. When anchored to the broader Christian tradition, we can see that "Apocalypse" is nothing to be stopped or survived. The word does not mean "akin to a dystopian movie," but an "unveiling," peering behind appearances to what's really there. The actual Apocalypse starts with disillusionment. The Revelation to John ends with a vision of a renewed cosmos, of "everything sad coming untrue," but it starts, remember, with a rebuke from the risen Christ to seven churches in Asia Minor for their lack of conformity to the gospel. The primary problem, the revelation said, was that their situation was unconscious to them. One church believed itself to be poor when it was really rich (Rev. 2:9), while another believed itself to be rich, prosperous, and in need of nothing, "not realizing that you are wretched, pitiable, poor, blind, and naked" (Rev. 3:17). To another church, perhaps eerily consistent with our present American moment, the risen Christ said, "You have the reputation of being alive, but you are dead. Wake up, and strengthen what remains and is about to die" (Rev. 3: 1–2).

In many evangelical Christian homes and churches in the twentieth century, a kitschy painting often hung of (a thoroughly Caucasian and Americanized) Jesus standing outside a door, with his hand stretching out to knock. This imagery comes from the Apocalypse, specifically from the message Jesus sent to the disobedient church at Laodicea: "Behold, I stand at the door and knock. If anyone hears my voice and opens the door, I will come in to him and eat with him, and he with me" (Rev. 3:20). Again, in individualized, hyperdemocratic ways, evangelicals often pictured this verse as Jesus standing outside the individual heart, waiting patiently for the individual sinner to invite Jesus into his or her heart. "Time after time, he has waited before, and now he is waiting again," the revivalist gospel song went, "to see if you're willing to open the door; O how he wants to come in!" This imagery is rightly critiqued since, first of all, Jesus' presence here is far more authoritative than that, but also because the message here is to a church, to a corporate body of believers. The evangelical imagery is not wholly wrong, though, and it points at something we might otherwise miss. Jesus is speaking to the church, but not only to the church. He is speaking there also to *persons*—to "anyone" who hears his voice, to anyone who can discern "what the Spirit says to the churches" (Rev. 3:22). Let your disillusion prompt you to listen.

Recognize Judgment. Usually if one hears an evangelical Christian referencing Jesus' cleansing of the temple, it's best to walk backward out of the room slowly. The verse—with Jesus taking up a whip and turning over the tables of the moneychangers in the temple courts—is used to justify almost any kind of quarrelsomeness and meanness imaginable. And yet, this account actually proves the reverse. What is striking about the passage is how rare it is for Jesus to act this way—given that he seems almost preternaturally calm in almost every circumstance recorded, even those in which everyone else seems to be panicking. On a boat near capsizing in a storm, Jesus sleeps. When arrested, Jesus calmly walks forward to identify himself. When standing trial before Pilate, he responds with a quiet gentleness. Here, though, in the temple courts, we see something we rarely see—Jesus visibly angry. Seeing the traders in the court there, Jesus seemed to be in meltdown, undoubtedly confusing to the merchants who were routinely in that very place. The disciples too must have been puzzled: why was someone imperturbable about people conspiring to kill him now flashing with rage about something so utterly unremarkable? After all, the marketplace had sold animals for sacrifice all throughout Jesus' lifetime, noted even in the account of his presentation in the temple right after his birth. Jesus, though, could see a crisis of integrity there. He said, "Is it not written, 'My house shall be called a house of prayer for all the nations'? But you have made it a den of robbers'" (Mark. 11:17). The lack of integrity was both vertical ("a house of prayer") and horizontal ("for all the nations").

When Jesus indicted the temple with becoming a "den of robbers," he was citing a warning from the prophet Jeremiah to Jerusalem: "Don't be fooled by those who promise you safety simply because the LORD's Temple is here . . . Do you really think you can steal, murder, commit adultery, lie, and burn incense to Baal and all those other new gods of yours, and then come here and stand before me in my Temple and chant, 'We are safe!'—only to go right back to all those evils again?" (Jer. 7:4, 9–10 NLT). Jeremiah told the people of Israel to look at the desolation of Shiloh, where the presence of God once was, to see that he could do the same to his temple. This old warning, and Jesus' dramatic enactment of it, ought to give us a pause.

In the temple, there might have been financial abuses, but the central issue seems to be the turning of what was meant to be sacred space into something "useful"—commerce. And, along with that, the space taken up was that of the most marginal and vulnerable people—the "outsiders" in the Court of the Gentiles in which those coming to pray were forced to do so in the middle of marketplace buzz. As one biblical scholar notes, Jesus here once again upended expectations of what a Messiah should do. The one who was expected to clear the temple of outsiders, aliens, and foreigners, instead ends up clearing out temple space *for* them. This is hardly a matter of ancient history, if the church is, as the Bible tells us, the temple of the living God, made up of living stones. Evangelicalism is just a "movement," but it claims to be a movement seeking renewal for the church. We must remember how Jesus responds to temples. We also cannot claim that answering a crisis of authenticity is somehow a distraction from our central task. Jesus' actions in the temple were not a detour from his trek to the cross, but the very path he took to get there. In John's account, Jesus is quoted as saying, citing Psalm 69:9, "Zeal for your house will consume me" (John. 2:17). This would prove to be true quite literally, as the tearing apart of this area of the temple would lead to Jesus himself torn apart on a Roman stake. Jesus overturned the status quo, and spoke of building the temple anew, a claim so shocking it was repeated as one of the charges of blasphemy and political disloyalty for which he would stand trial on the way to the Place of the Skull. In the overturned tables, the people thought that Jesus was violating God's temple when, in fact, his zeal for that temple led to anger at what it had become. They thought he was "losing his religion" in the theological sense, but he was losing his religion in the southern folk-language sense. But we should also notice the aftermath of this moment of controversy in the life of Jesus. Matthew records that immediately afterward the blind and the lame, those on the margins of society, came to Jesus and were healed. The children in the temple courts started to cry out "Hosanna to the Son of David!" To this, the religious leaders "were indignant" and sought to quiet them (Matt. 21:14–17). The crisis would lead to a renewed focus on the gospel itself: that the mission is not for the confident insiders, but for those who seem for the moment to be rejected and powerless, those who do not seem to be "useful." Stop right now, and ask who those people are—the people your tribe would like you to keep invisible. Pay attention to them. Embody a credible witness for them.

You can't choose whether you will experience apocalypse. But an apocalypse can be an Armageddon or an invitation. Choose the latter. You can't choose whether you will be disillusioned, you can only choose when you will be disillusioned. Choose now.

And ask, as your illusions fall, what it is that God wants you to see. It might be that, through your tears, you can't see that the gardener in the graveyard with you is the One whose absence you are grieving. That's disillusionment too. You can decide to lose your illusions that way, in order to see something that is not visible, but is nonetheless real. And, with that, we can choose to be the people who embody a credible gospel, a gospel that is more than an illusion, more than a useful means to some end. Somewhere out there there's at least one disillusioned fifteen-year-old, losing his religion, who needs to see that. Maybe his life depends on it. Maybe yours does too.

CHAPTER TWO

LOSING OUR AUTHORITY

How the Truth Can Save Us from Tribalism

Two words filled me with rage: *Jesus saves.* On January 6, 2021, the president of the United States assembled a mob in Washington—promising a "wild" time—and told them to march to the Capitol in order to halt the constitutional process for the United States Congress to certify a presidential election the president insisted, falsely, had been stolen from him. The mob tore through barricades, broke through windows and doors, beat police officers with flagpoles and fire extinguishers. Some chanted "Hang Mike Pence" as others constructed a makeshift gallows in order to do just that—believing the vice president of the United States to be a traitor based on what President Trump had just told them, that Pence had the power to unilaterally overturn the election. American flags were thrown down and replaced with Trump and Confederate flags. Congressional leaders hid while the doors buckled from mobs seeking to attack them. And there, held aloft over the churning horde of people, was a sign—"Jesus Saves." That the two messages, a gallows and "Jesus Saves" could coexist is a sign of crisis for American Christianity.

Some dismissed the Christian symbolism at the insurrection—not only the signs but also the prayers "in Jesus' name" right next to a horn-wearing pagan shaman in the well of the evacuated United States Senate among many other things. And yet, the January 6 rally-turned-riot was preceded in the days before it by the "Jericho March," at which Christian musicians played worship songs while well-known evangelical speakers repeated the same falsehoods that led to the violence—that the election was stolen, and that this was a moment of "spiritual warfare." One might think that this use of Christian symbolism was a momentary enthusiasm that would "cool off" given time. But by Christmas, Donald Trump was in the pulpit at the First Baptist Church of Dallas, Texas—at one time one of the most significant and influential congregations in American evangelical Christianity—giving a political speech as the congregation chanted "USA! USA!" Now, granted, this church is not representative in many ways. They wrote and performed an anthem literally called "Make America Great Again," and the pastor was well known for defending any Trump statement (when, in yet another act of racial signaling, Trump called a group of mostly Black nations "shithole countries," the pastor did say that he wished the president's language had been cleaner). But this is not as much of an outlier as I might hope. Survey after survey showed alarming numbers of white evangelicals believed the lie that mobilized the mobs—that a vast left-wing conspiracy (somehow including the conservative Republican governors and election officials in Arizona and Georgia) stole a presidential election. And, even worse, alarming numbers of white evangelicals tell pollsters they believe that violence might be necessary in the future.

If this were limited to threats on American democracy, the situation would be dire enough, but church after church is divided over conspiracy theories and falsehoods. Some of them are related to politics, but many aren't. Journalist Tim Alberta chronicled the ways that some pastors have leveraged the political fixations and extremist positions of the present moment to build churches, leaving other pastors—those who went into the ministry for reasons quite distant from politics and showmanship—"feeling trapped." As Alberta puts it, "One stray remark could split their congregation, or even cost them their job. Yet a strictly apolitical approach can be counterproductive; their unwillingness to engage only invites more scrutiny. The whisper campaigns brand conservative pastors as moderate, and moderate pastors as Marxists. In this environment, a church leader's stance on biblical inerrancy is less important than whether he is considered 'woke.' His command of Scripture is less relevant than suspicions about how he voted in the last election."* Much of what we experience as conspiracy theories

---

*Tim Alberta, "How Politics Poisoned the Church," *The Atlantic*, June 2022, 33.

now is far beyond what we've experienced in the past—the man in your Bible study who thinks there might be something to the second shooter at the grassy knoll or the woman who suspects that the pyramid with the eye on the back of the dollar bill is a secret message from a Satanist cabal. What we see now is more than crackpottery but a weaponized ideology that has led to the deaths of people, and probably will lead to the deaths of many more to come.

The irony of the present crisis is that evangelical Christians in the United States have viewed ourselves as those who hold to "objective truth" over and against a kind of deconstructionist relativism. We came out of the fundamentalist side of the controversies over biblical authority in the mainline Protestant denominations of the fractious 1920s, and the concept of the truthfulness of the Bible implies the existence of actual "truth"—objective realities that are not merely generated by a community. Ruth Graham at the *New York Times* observed that the American evangelical drive toward conspiracy theory and propaganda was at least partially fueled by the global COVID-19 pandemic in which people were disconnected from their actual embodied church communities and regularly both consumed information and found alternative "communities" online. After the lockdowns were over, and people began to return to church, the divisions and arguments—whether over public health or politics or race in the aftermath of the George Floyd murder— showed that many evangelicals were radicalized, and that many Christians did not have a common set of "facts" or a common concept of "truth" with which to adjudicate these controversies. She is partially right, though the pandemic (and the 2016 and 2020 elections) accelerated these trends but did not create them.

Increasingly, in this sort of American culture, it is not just that we are divided about what we value about the way things should be, but what we are allowed to say about the way things actually are. Now, notice, what I wrote here is not what we *see* about the way things are, but what we are *allowed to say*. This is because we live in a time in which "truth" is seen as a means to tribal belonging, rather than as a reality that exists outside of us. And that's true even among, sometimes even especially among, those who spent the last twenty years arguing about the dangers of postmodern relativistic ideas of "truth" and the "rejection of metanarratives." Now, "objectivity" of truth has often been oversimplified. On many important things, we see, the apostle Paul writes, "through a glass, darkly" (1 Cor. 13:12 KJV). Our passions and experiences and intuitions often warp the way we see things, especially the most important things, which is why we need grace. People are going to have—from now till the Apocalypse—arguments about what is true and what is false, what is real and what is fake. Our problem now, though, is that, increasingly, we are called not just to argue about what is true, but to say things that we *know* to be false, just to prove that we are part of the tribe to which we belong.

Some would consider an evangelical Christian criticizing one's "own side" to be acting disloyally and hurting the unity of the church. These anti-jeremiad Jeremiahs would make sense if the people issuing them weren't strongly denouncing dangers and errors in the outside culture—often on matters where there's almost no controversy among conservative evangelicals. They want jeremiads against the abortion culture or "sexual anarchy" or New Atheism or gender ideology. And most of those—at least in the more conservative tribe of evangelicalism—are, and have always been, just as clear on those matters as on those of racial injustice or sexual abuse cover-ups or political captivity, often more so than those who seem to want culture wars right up to the point that they affect our kind of churches. We should not critique evangelicalism (at least not in public), we are told, because to do so would be to curry favor with "the elites." And yet, which in fact curries favor: Saying to the world that evangelical Christianity is true and beautiful enough that we shouldn't betray our own stated ideals? Or saying to populist masses (and donors): we will speak loudly on the issues with which you agree with us, and remain silent or dismiss as "distractions" those you don't? We will attack with force those politicians and cultural movements that virtually none of our evangelical audience supports, while finding ways to justify those they do? This is just another way of sacrificing the future for those we fear in the present. And it's another way of replacing a commitment to truth with the shibboleths of a tribe.

Where does this eclipse of truth lead? Actually, the path is not toward the anarchy of "follow your heart," at least not in the long run. "In those days there was no king in Israel," the book of Judges tells us. "Everyone did what was right in his own eyes" (Judg. 21:25). In the short term, this led to chaos and disorder, but the chaos and disorder led ultimately to the clamoring for a "king over us" so that "we also may be like all the nations, and that our king may judge us and go out before us and fight our battles" (1 Sam. 8: 19–20). And here we are. The political scientist Jonathan Rauch argues that what's at stake in this hour is not just the diminishment of facts, but something he calls the "constitution of knowledge," the most basic commonality of truth required for life together. And one plank of that "constitution" is the principle of "no personal authority."* Obviously, I disagree with Rauch, an atheist, about the ultimate application of this principle since I believe in the personal authority of Jesus of Nazareth. When he says, "But I say unto you . . ." I go with him. But that's because I believe that Jesus of Nazareth is not just a teacher or a guru, but the Son of God, the Word made flesh, the one in whom the entire cosmos holds together. But Rauch is right when it comes to merely human authority. Without at least some common standard of basic truth, life together—whether in a neighborhood, a church, or a nation—is impossible. Questions become not about what is true or false, but rather how to prove that one is really in one's tribe. When the claims of an individual or a group cannot be questioned without the possibility of exile, and when exile becomes the worst fate imaginable, we are in a place of confusion. Such confusion evaporates the reasons why, for instance, we want doctors to rely on studies and data before treating illnesses rather than, "Well,

---

*Jonathan Rauch, *The Constitution of Knowledge: A Defense of Truth* (Washington, DC: Brookings Institution Press, 2021), 89–92.

my Aunt Flossie chewed a little bit of rat poison every morning and she never got dementia, so . . ."

Demagogues and authoritarians know that a "post-truth" environment is precisely where they will thrive. What's especially concerning is the rate at which strongmen and authoritarians—in North America and around the world—count on the support of evangelical Christians. In some ways, as with other aspects of this moment, it might be that many evangelical Christians don't recognize authoritarianism because the petri dish for authoritarian experiments has often been evangelical churches. When we see example after example of bullying, intimidating leaders in such high-profile positions in evangelical Christianity, the question is often posed, "Why do people flock to this, and why do they put up with it?" Such people are often told they are looking for authority and will find it wherever they can get it. There's a certain sense in which that's accurate, but a much larger sense in which it is not. The draw to authoritarianism (of various kinds—Left and Right, theistic and atheistic) is not actually because people want authority but because they do *not*. The relationship between authority and authoritarianism, after all, is not a matter of taking legitimate authority and multiplying it any more than polytheism is just *more* monotheism or polyamory is just *more* monogamy. The worship of many gods is a repudiation and a contradiction of the worship of one God. Sex with multiple partners is a repudiation and a contradiction of marital love. And authoritarianism—whether in a national or global movement or within the small places of a church or a family dinner table—is a repudiation and contradiction of authority.

Comparative religion scholar Tara Isabella Burton identifies what she calls "the new atavists"—a concept that ranges from the "manosphere" of anti–politically correct masculinists on YouTube to the Alt-Right and those adjacent to them—are far more similar to their counterparts on the Left than they would want to admit. "Although they may valorize authority in the abstract, in practice they are obsessed with tearing down 'the cathedral': the institutions, from universities to media companies, that foment the ideological orthodoxy of contemporary progressive society."* A similar phenomenon is found in Christian circles with the so-called "theo-bros," who think they are the opposite of the hyperdeconstructing exvangelical firebrands, but who share the very same "aren't we naughty?" ethos. What becomes the source of authority in these cases is not the persuasive appeals or the moral credibility of those speaking but their willingness to brawl and to transgress norms in ways that can seem shocking. Civility, then, is surrender. Empathy is sin. Love of neighbor is "liberal." Justice is "Marxism." With this comes the need to rally around someone who will prove his (almost always "his") alpha status by railing against the enemies—and even against his followers—in ways that can reassure the tribe, "My home-church pastor would *hate* this!" Those who meet this need

---

*Tara Isabella Burton, *Strange Rites: New Religions for a Godless World* (New York: PublicAffairs, 2020), 211.

can—and often do—demand accelerating levels of authority over the churches or movements built around them, just as political leaders who follow the same playbook do.

When one recognizes this sort of abusive authoritarianism, the first impulse is often to reject the very idea of authority, even as those harmed by institutions sometimes find it almost impossible to trust any institution ever again. This flight from authority, though, only leads to another kind of authoritarian, promising to protect one against authoritarians, if one will just surrender some agency and thought and follow the reactionary pull. That happens within nations and states, but it can also happen in a family or in a church.

What a movement rooted in power instead of truth actually wants are people who are willing to accept seemingly crazy ideas . . . and to change them at a moment's notice, not because they've been persuaded by some other idea, but just because the talking points have changed. That's what George Orwell warned about in totalitarian states. "It sets up unquestionable dogmas, and it alters them from day to day," he wrote. "It needs the dogmas, because it needs absolute obedience from its subjects, but it can't avoid the changes, which are dictated by the needs of power politics."* Today, you are asked to be enraged about the secret pedophile ring in a pizza parlor, but tomorrow, when this is proved not to be true and the purveyors of it move on to something else, no one apologizes or announces a change of mind. It's just forgotten. The language wasn't

---

*George Orwell, "Literature and Totalitarianism," 1941.

actually a truth claim, but a means to an end—to show you who is one of us and who isn't, who belongs and who doesn't.

The antidote to authoritarianism is authority itself, rightly defined. The sociologist Robert Nisbet correctly differentiated between *authority* and *power*. He defined *power* as "something external and based upon force," while *authority* is rooted in persuasion and allegiance. Authority does not bully or intimidate with raw force but is rooted in vital social relationships and to truths more transcendent than the will-to-power or the force of a personality. "Power arises only when authority breaks down," Nisbet argued.* Media analyst Martin Gurri argues that the fracturing we see all around us is exactly what one would expect after a loss of authority, which he defines as the legitimacy of being able to tell a shared story. "What passes for authority is devolving into the political war-band and the online mob—that is, to the shock troops of populism, left and right," he writes. "Deprived of a legitimate authority to interpret events and settle factual disputes, we fly apart from each other—or rather, we flee into our own heads, into a subjectivized existence. We assume ornate and exotic identities, and bear them in the manner of those enormous wigs once worn at Versailles."† Left in the wake of this, he contends, is the institution that "clings to life and

---

*Robert Nisbet, *The Quest for Community: A Study in the Ethics of Order and Freedom* (San Francisco: Institute for Contemporary Studies, 1990), xxvi.

†Martin Gurri, *The Revolt of the Public and the Crisis of Authority in the New Millennium* (San Francisco: Stripe, 2018), 396.

still wields power, but has been bled dry of legitimacy. It has no true authority or prestige in the eyes of the public, and it survives by a precarious combination of inertia and the public's unwillingness to provide an alternative. It exists by default."* He means such institutions as the old political party structures, but could there be a better description of the Christian denominations in American life right now?

This, of course, has religious implications. Think of the authority versus power debate as the difference between "Baal is the rain god; worship him and avoid drought" and "I am the Lord your God, the God of your fathers Abraham and Isaac and Jacob." One is based on the fear of retaliation from a stronger power; the other on a covenant with a God who is worthy of heart allegiance and who speaks truth. Jesus spoke with "authority, and not as the scribes" (Mark 1:22). That meant that Jesus spoke the truth, but it meant more than that. He also carried personal credibility. He could be trusted, not just with the facts of the moment but with everything going forward. That kind of authority is not about enforcing conformity. Jesus asks of those attempting to follow him, "What are you seeking?" (John 1:38). In that, there is wisdom, gravity, affection, and knowledge. The result of that—for those who are seeking—is our agreement, in our own lives, with Jesus' mother at the wedding of Cana, "Do whatever he tells you" (John. 2:5). That's not only because we

---

*Ibid., 290.

have found whatever he says to be true (although that's certainly the case), but because we trust *him*, in what we can see and in what we cannot. Authority rests on the integrity of the source.

Fred Rogers, a pioneering children's television broadcaster of the twentieth century was asked in one of the last interviews of his career whether he was offended by all the various parodies of him performed on late-night comedy shows and elsewhere. Only once, Rogers said, and that was with a local network's afternoon comedy sketch hour in which a comedian, dressed in Rogers's distinctive cardigan sweater and sneakers combination and mimicking Rogers's trademark gentle "hi neighbor" voice, said, "Now children, take your mother's hairspray and your daddy's cigarette lighter, and press the buttons, and you'll have a blowtorch."* The parody was done for adults and for laughs, of course, but the real Mr. Rogers believed that one could never know when a child might see it. That was when at least one comedian learned that Mr. Rogers could master a cease-and-desist letter. The problem was not just that this man might be teaching children to become arsonists (though that would be bad enough), but that he was doing so in the guise of Mr. Rogers. He was leveraging the trust and reputation built over a

---

*Fred Rogers, "I've Got the Greatest Job in the World," interview by Karen Herman, The Interviews: An Oral History of Television, Television Academy Foundation, July 22, 1999, in *Fred Rogers: The Last Interview and Other Conversations* (Brooklyn: Melville House, 2021), 55.

lifetime for something that could possibly tip from a cartoonish comedy to a (literally) incendiary tragedy.

Whether referencing racism, nationalism, political identity, uncovered scandal, or any other crisis within the American church, people often ask, "What does this do to the gospel?" My answer is always the same: "Nothing." Nothing, that is, if what we mean by the gospel is that, as the Bible puts it, "in Christ God was reconciling the world to himself" (2 Cor. 5:19). But what one asking that question usually means is, "What do these things do to the credibility of the church's witness to the gospel?" That's a different question. That's a question about the blowtorch. Now Jesus is not Mister Rogers; Aslan is not a tame lion, and so forth. But the alarm about the credibility of one trusted, exploited for other ends—whether malicious or just trivial—is the same, except of infinitely more importance. Consider, for instance, sexual abuse, an act that in any context and by any institution is a grave atrocity. How much worse is it when this horror is committed—or is covered up—not just by leveraging personal or institutional trust but by using the very name of Jesus to carry out such wickedness, against those he has shown repeatedly that he loves and values? When sexual abuse happens within a church, violence is added to violence—sexual, physical, emotional, and spiritual. Predators know this power is great, which is why predators and would-be authoritarians use even the most beautiful concepts—grace or forgiveness or Matthew 18 or the life of David—to cover up their crimes or as weapons to victimize the vulnerable. And that's why institutions seeking to protect themselves will take on the name of Jesus, in order to say that victims, survivors, or whistleblowers are compromising "the mission" or creating "disunity in the Body" when they point out the horrors behind the veil. This—not "cussing"—is what the Bible means when it says, "Do not take the name of the Lord your God in vain."

So what can you do as you stand and stay in a post-truth culture?

Maintain Attention. It's one of the hardest things to do in a whirl of constant information and, probably even more so, in a time of constant anxiety. A generation ago, historian Mark Noll, examining American evangelical populism, entrepreneurialism, and anti-intellectualism, wrote of what he called "the scandal of the evangelical mind," the scandal being that there isn't much of an evangelical mind.* While the Noll thesis certainly holds up, I almost long for the days when we could have the luxury of worrying about the evangelical mind. Right now it seems to me that we face a problem more primal than that of the intellect. We face the scandal of the evangelical limbic system. Many have grown up in churches rooted primarily in fear of hell—with "Judgment Houses" at Halloween reenacting torments of damnation or sermons intended to viscerally tap into a sense of panic about one's eternal condition. Since I believe, with Jesus, that hell actually exists, the warnings themselves—if carried out in counterproductive ways—were at least focused on what should prompt genuine alarm.

---

*Mark Noll, *The Scandal of the Evangelical Mind* (Grand Rapids: Eerdmans, 1994).

The evangelical culture of the past half century has focused comparatively little on judgment for the hearer, and much more on a different kind of fear—the imminent threat from one's neighbors or culture. This coincides with a similar state of felt emergency in almost every area of American life, accelerated dramatically by social media technology. Not long ago, I spoke with a Silicon Valley tech expert who has spent years examining social media polarization. Though not a Christian, she recognized how vulnerable churches could be to the spreading of misinformation and disinformation, and made the point that nothing is accidental about the way radical and crazed content gets traction. The algorithms recognize, she said, how emotions work. Emotions such as affection or wonder or curiosity don't prompt people to linger on posts—much less to spread them. But anger and fear do. The technology exploits the element of fallen human psychology—what she would call "the lizard brain" or the "reptilian" part of the brain—that is alert to threats and danger, and that tweaking the technology is a small component of the problem over against what can't be changed—that part of the human condition.

This is especially toxic when merged with religious identity. The church feels afraid of extinction, and then makes alliances with whomever they believe can protect them. That's not unusual in history at all. As a matter of fact, God is consistently condemning this fear motive for such alliances—whether with Egypt or Assyria or elsewhere. God even repudiates the people of God managing fear by mimicking the tough-image stances of those nations—by relying on their numbers or their armaments or their storehouses of wealth. A religious leader can always assuage a conscience by convincing himself that the alternative is worse. The church leaders also—even those who aren't already nationalist ideologues—sometimes get on board with shilling for the state if they are afraid of what the rulers can do to them personally. Every "king" has "court prophets." The prophet Micaiah was told, "Behold, the words of the prophets with one accord are favorable to the king. Let your word be like the word of one of them, and speak favorably" (1 Kings 22:13). In other words, everyone else is on board; you get there too. King Jeroboam and the priest Amaziah delivered a very clear word to the prophet Amos when Amos's prophecies were not affirming of the king: "Never again prophesy at Bethel, for it is the king's sanctuary, and it is a temple of the kingdom" (Amos 7:13). God, of course, saw it differently.

And, maybe most often of all, religious leaders fear their own people. The religious leaders of Jesus' day repeatedly held back the full expression of their thoughts because Jesus and John the Baptist were popular with the crowds. Later, these religious leaders made alliances even with political forces they hated (the Roman client state) in order to keep the people from following after a leader the state saw as a threat to stability and the religious leaders saw as a threat to their power. Whether from favor or fear or fear of losing favor, the real motivating force for any church is atheism—the most pernicious kind of atheism, that which thinks it believes in God.

You cannot change the human condition, and you cannot change the technological or cultural ecosystem in which you live and move and have your being. But you can *be changed*. And you will need to be. Simone Weil warned about what happens to attention when everything is politicized by a party system. Those systems come with penalties. "These penalties extend into all areas of life: career, affection, friendship, reputation, the external aspect of honor, sometimes even family life," she wrote. "The Communist Party has developed this system to perfection." Even for those who don't sacrifice their inner integrity for such a system, she warned, a change can happen even without their noticing it. She gave the example of a person attempting to calculate complex mathematical equations in a context in which he knows "that he will be flogged every time he obtains an even number as a result." For most people—even strong and courageous people—something inside them will start inducing them to "give a slight twist to the calculations, in order to obtain an odd number at the end." In such a situation, their attention is divided and compromised, and they may not even know it.*

Gospel Christianity tells us that there is, in fact, something that can change the reptilian mind—and that our brains have faced reptiles for a long, long time. The serpent, after all, was the most cunning of all the beasts of the field that the Lord God had made (Gen. 3:1). The old reptile of Eden appealed to our human appetites, to

---

*Simone Weil, *On the Abolition of All Political Parties*, trans. Simon Leys (New York: New York Review Books, 2013), 22–23.

our perceived autonomy, summoned a fear of mortality, and then offered a "fix" for it. In the biblical storyline, the hyperrational coolness of the snake at the beginning is matched by the limbic hotness later on. The ancient dragon rages all the more "because he knows that his time is short" (Rev. 12:12). Looking at the plight of fallen humanity, honestly, in any age, could lead to a kind of pessimistic despair. After all, what can one do about human nature? This is dangerous because it is a subconscious way of tossing aside the supernatural. It's a sign that we are secularizing. People do this in many different ways. We can do it through a kind of hand-wringing anxiety that looks at the current reality in the people we know, or the church itself, and assume a gloomy version of "tomorrow will be like today, only more so" (Isa. 56:12 NASB). Or we can do it through a kind of "If you can't beat them, join them" cynicism that we can deceive ourselves is "realism" and "the way things are."

Or, maybe even worst of all, we can find a gospel "realistic" enough for these times—with the kind of half gospel that activates the amygdala rather than one that lightens the conscience. For some of us that resignation comes from a fear of the so-called lizard brain in what we perceive to be "the world." How do we keep from upsetting those whose hostility could, we think, hurt us? For others that resignation is a way to exploit the lizard brain of our own people—how do we frighten them to the point that we can "lead" them, and how can we find ways to sanctify what the Bible calls "works of the flesh" of wrath, rancor, rage, and fear, so that they not only don't bother our consciences but so we can actually see them as the only realistic way forward and, in fact, as themselves signs of Christian conviction?

The way that we step away from all this is to recognize that it's happening, that we are vulnerable to it. When we don't expect the Spirit to be able to give life, to grant us the mind of Christ, to crucify the works of the flesh, and to bring to life the fruit of the Spirit, then we don't call for it, we don't long for it, we don't pray for it, we don't model it. And then a lifeless but furious church leads to people who start to wonder if "born again" is just a way to say, "people whose lizard brains light up in Red state ways rather than Blue state ways" (or vice versa). The first step to becoming a people of truth is to recognize what makes us afraid, and to ask why and who benefits from that fear.

Tell the Truth. By that I don't mean you should dismantle all the lies around you. You can't do that. But you can discipline yourself toward personal honesty. That starts with realizing that bearing false witness is a sin, and that lying distorts not just the truth but *us.* Those of us who have embraced the gospel did so by confessing that we are sinners and, more specifically, that we are liars. In the letter to the Romans, the apostle Paul wrote about God's holy judgment on "deceit" and ruthlessness. That includes those who know "God's decree" on sin but nonetheless not only do such sins themselves but also "give approval to those who practice them" (Rom. 1:32). In establishing the sin that God judges, Paul wrote of those who "use their tongues to deceive" as well as those whose "feet are swift to shed blood" (Rom. 3:13–15). The apostle likewise wrote: "Let God be true though every one were a liar" (Rom. 3:4). And to those who suggest that "if through my lie God's truth abounds to his glory, why am I still being condemned as a sinner?" Paul charged them with "slander" and said that "their condemnation is just" (Rom. 3:7–8). He warned about those who would serve "their own appetites, and by smooth talk and flattery" deceive "the hearts of the naive" (Rom. 16:18).

"To knowingly pretend a lie is true is, simply put, to lie," wrote Yuval Levin in light of the propaganda about a stolen election. "Doing that carefully enough to let you claim you're only raising questions only makes it even clearer that you know you're lying. Lying to people is no way to speak for them or represent them. It is a way of showing contempt for them, and of using them rather than being useful to them."* He is precisely right in every part of that assertion. To pretend a lie is true is to lie. What's at stake for a country is bad enough, but what's at stake for the church is even greater. The gospel, though, does not go forward by propaganda or demagoguery or by cynical appeals to popular conspiracy theories or folk religion. The gospel goes forth, the apostle Paul asserted, not with "underhanded ways" or with "cunning," but by the "open statement of the truth" (2 Cor. 4:2). The witness goes forward, he wrote, through "truthful speech" that is demonstrated "by purity, knowledge, pa-

*Yuvan Levin, "Failures of Leadership in a Populist Age," *National Review*, January 4, 2021.

tience, kindness, the Holy Spirit, genuine love" (2 Cor. 6:6–7). All this is necessary, the apostle asserted, precisely because this is a "day of salvation," the moment of decision, and therefore we should "put no obstacle in anyone's way" (2 Cor 6:1–3). The popular revivalist distinction of "heart knowledge" from "head knowledge" could, and sometimes has, ended up in anti-intellectualism or sentimentalism, but the distinction was getting at something real and essential. The gospel appeals to the mind, the affections, the imagination, and the conscience, not to the limbic system. The gospel does not seek to depersonalize people into a faceless crowd of channeled anger.

The problem within the nation, the church, and the culture is not so much that people fall for crazed and irrational conspiracy theories. The problem is that too many people who don't actually believe the things they are saying say them anyway, because they are afraid of the people who believe such things. Notice how this happens. The argument is that we need grown-ups in the room. As one politician once put it, "Someone who is five steps in front of his people is a leader; someone who is ten steps in front of his people is a martyr." People in the vortex of craziness—whether in a workplace or in a church or in a government—tell themselves they have to play along with things they find insane in order to maintain their ability, long-term, to keep bad things from happening. "If I'm not here, someone worse will be," they reason. There's a kernel of truth there, of course. I would put my head in my hand every time I would hear about a young pastor, after just arriving at a church, removing the American flag from the sanctuary or trying to ex-communicate everybody who hadn't been to church in a year. "Even if you are right, these are not your biggest problems right now," I would say. "And this is the wrong time to take them on." Daniel in Babylon was willing to go to the lion's den over the demand that he worship the emperor, but when it came to eating the rich delicacies of the king's table, he prudently posed alternatives instead. Jesus didn't believe he owed the temple tax, but paid it "not to give offense to them" (Matt. 17:27). The apostle Paul circumcised Timothy so that the younger man's Gentile heritage wouldn't be a stumbling block to the mission (Acts 16:3). The problem is that there comes a point where one moves from "choosing battles" to the searing of a conscience. Peter's refusal to eat with the Gentiles was, Paul wrote, "not in step with the truth of the gospel" (Gal. 2:14). Almost every time someone acts out of fear of getting kicked out of their tribe, the person reasons that this is just "working within the system" or "living to fight another day."

On the way up, we tell ourselves, "I don't have the platform yet to speak; when I get one, I will." After we arrive wherever we were heading, we tell ourselves, "I have too much to lose; if I am not at the table, they will lose my voice." We think this is the voice of prudence inside of us, but maybe, more often than not, it's just ambition mixed with fear. Not only are the internal rationalizations circular, though, so are the external circumstances. Whether in a church or a ministry workplace or a city council or a neighborhood association, we tell ourselves, "I am going to live with this little bit of craziness so that I will be here to stop major craziness." While those crazy things are happening, someone watching all this is looking around wondering, "Am I the only one who sees this is crazy?" When everyone else acts like whatever the situation might be is normal, that observer shrugs and concludes, "It must just be me." And then whatever the craziness is becomes the new normal. And folks "conserve their influence" for when it's needed, for whatever is just a step crazier than that. I've been there, and that way leads to nowhere good. Sooner or later one's influence isn't conserved, but hoarded. Sooner or later, one is operating not out of prudent patience but from a seared conscience.

You, though, can dissent from that way, and the first step is to simply stop speaking things as true that you don't actually believe. And when you change your mind, do so on the basis of persuasion, or even of repentance, not on the basis of what it takes to stay within the tribe, or to prove one's identity, or to keep from being bullied or intimidated. To say that we are to be trusted for truth is not to mean, as it has sometimes meant in the past, that we are searching for endless and ever-narrowing heresy trials for the sake of "truth." It means instead that we recognize Jesus' words that, for each of us personally, "out of the abundance of the heart the mouth speaks" (Matt. 12:34). The way of Christ demands an integrity, a "holding together" of the inner and the outer, of what one believes to be true internally and what one says publicly. This is what it means to "Let your 'yes' be yes and your 'no' be no" (James 5:12; see also Matt. 5:37).

We can see why this inner/outer, mind/heart integrity matters from our very first response of faith. The apostle Paul wrote that "if you confess with your mouth that Jesus is Lord and believe in your heart that God raised him from the dead, you will be saved" (Rom. 10:9). In repentance, we both sorrow over our sins and we confess them (1 John 1:9). The result of a lack of sincerity and honesty is not just that we deceive others but that "we deceive ourselves, and the truth is not in us" (1 John 1:8). A conscience unhinged from sincerity and truth-telling ends up unable to distinguish a lie from the truth and "will go on from bad to worse, deceiving and being deceived" (2 Tim. 3:13). Watch yourself and notice when you start believing things not on the basis of their reality or unreality, but their usefulness. If Jesus is, in fact, not just the carrier of truth, but the Truth, in person, then your relationship with truth is not just about a well-ordered democracy or even a well-ordered church (although it's essential for both), but about your own personal interaction with Jesus.

Avoid Foolish Controversies. Everything you say should be true, but that doesn't mean you should say everything that is true. Paul told Timothy, "Have nothing to do with foolish, ignorant controversies; you know that they breed quarrels" (2 Tim. 2:23). Jesus recognized when his opponents were seeking to "trap him in his talk" (Mark 12:13) and would refuse to engage in such controversies on the terms this kind of people were setting. Sometimes he would answer a question directly. Often he would reframe the question, ask a different question, or just leave. This is especially difficult for those who have had family members—often parents—radicalized by disinformation or conspiracy theories. You do not have the responsibility to undo all that. As a matter of fact, in many cases, one of the strongest antidotes to the pull of such propaganda is to maintain a connection with people who are lonely and aching for community or to make sense of their world.

Try saying: "You and we see things differently on this. We love you, and we want to see you. Can't we just leave the politics aside and talk about other things?" This isn't that big of an ask. We all do that all the time. I don't bring up cousin Ronnie's ex-girlfriend when I meet his new wife. I don't quote Hank Williams lyrics in front of friends I know to be recovering alcoholics. I don't talk about how much I dislike tuna casserole at the table with someone who just served it. Agreeing together on avoiding topics that would only cause discord is not lying about those matters. It's just agreeing that you like being with one another more than you value being proven right about those things. Is it possible that they will say no to all that, and that you cannot be around them if you don't accept their politics or their conspiracy theories in total? Sadly, it is, but, in most cases, that's not likely. But, again, you can only control your own attitude and actions, not theirs. The Bible tells us to "Strive for peace with everyone" (Heb. 12:14), and "If possible, so far as it depends on you, live peaceably with all" (Rom. 12:18).

Don't Self-Censor. Misinformation and disinformation can have effects far beyond those who actively believe the lies. The conspiracy theories have an effect even when the majority of people don't believe them. Very few people—in the church or in the world—are flat-earth conspiracy theorists of the sort who contend that the moon landing was a hoax filmed on a Hollywood production set. One pastor told me, though, of one family in his church who did. While 99 percent of the entire rest of the church believed the world to be round, the 99 percent didn't wake up in the morning energized by that question. The flat-earth family did. At first, people in this church did exactly what they did—they patiently bore with the flat-earth family. After all, the church is a household, in which we are to bear one another's burdens, and quirkiness can be one of the burdens we bear. Over time, though, the pastor noticed that he was self-censoring. He wouldn't preach a series on Joshua because he knew the passage where Joshua commanded the sun to stand still would prompt "See? The Bible is with us!" taunts from the flat-earth crew, and he was frankly too exhausted to spend an entire sermon explaining phenomenological language in Scripture. So he just preached through Ephesians instead. When the chair of the missions committee led the church in prayer, she would stop herself before saying, "Let's pray for our missionaries around the globe," because she didn't want emails questioning whether she was a secret liberal or whether she had ever considered what "the pillars of the earth" in the Bible have to do with a premodern three-story universe. Even without changing a single mind, the flat-earth family just wore everyone down. Meanwhile, the earth spun on, revolving around the sun like ever.

This is important because studies show that the extremist ranting we see all over social media right now is actually from a very small and unrepresentative number of people. That would appear to be good news, but it's not as good as it seems. The extreme voices, one scholar argues, start to dominate because they will do things the more balanced majority will not—like online harassment and personal attacks at worst, or, at best, they just keep pounding a matter until everyone else is exhausted by it all. More than that, he writes, the psychological dynamics are just different. The more extreme people opt for social media in the first place for different reasons than most people—for a sense of status and meaning in their lives. The more balanced people, he argues, just don't crave controversy the same way, and they have too much to lose. They really don't want to lose friendships or alienate family over something as meaningless as political opinions thrown out into cyberspace. They find purpose in places other than winning arguments with strangers so they just don't throw ideas out there when they don't want a vortex of constant back-and-forth afterward. What then ends up happening is a kind of "self-cancel-culture" as the emotionally and spiritually healthiest people mute themselves in order to go about their lives and not deal with the pressure from those for whom these arguments *are* their lives.*

That's about more than social media. This is precisely the dynamic that seems to be happening in church after church after church. Most people love Jesus and love one another, even when we exasperate one

*Chris Bail, *Breaking the Social Media Prism: How to Make Our Platforms Less Polarizing* (Princeton: Princeton University Press, 2021).

another. But a small group of people are driven by increasingly extreme grievances—and actually *like* church conflict. Here's how this becomes a critical problem. When congregational forums or denominational meetings turn into brawls over real or imagined (usually the latter) social media controversies, the people who were engaged because they believe in the mission start to step back, disengage, and live out their lives. They assume that the fever will break, eventually. It doesn't. The point in these situations is usually not about persuading the majority of people but, as Jonathan Rauch points out, on demoralizing people until they self-censor to the point of giving up.* And then the cycle is almost unbreakable. The church (or the political party or the neighborhood association or the family reunion) becomes a place blown about by every wind of conspiracy—until the ones who want to be there are those who want that. The Czech dissident and playwright Václav Havel famously wrote that "a single, seemingly powerless person who dares to cry out the word of truth and to stand behind it with all his person and all his life, ready to pay a high price, has surprisingly greater power, though formally disenfranchised, than do thousands of anonymous voters."† Have we not seen this to be true? If you self-censor at all, do an honest check with yourself. Are you

---

*Rauch, *Constitution of Knowledge*, 249.

†Václav Havel, *Open Letters: Selected Writings, 1965–1990*, ed. Paul Wilson (New York: Random House, 1991), 270.

withholding something out of love or out of fear? If the latter, abandon your timidity and tell the truth.

Question Authority. At first glance, this sounds like a slogan of the hippie counterculture of a half century ago or of the therapeutic age in which one must look inside one's own heart to find "your truth." That's not what I mean here. To hold to genuine authority is to be skeptical of other, competing claims to authority. To believe that there is such a thing as truth is to realize that not everything that claims to be truth is so, and that some such claims are dangerous. Psychologist and researcher Stanley Milgram pointed out that tests with human subjects reveal that, given an authority to obey and a community to which to belong, the individual human conscience can find "cover" to do things that even they would have found before to be morally repugnant. "A substantial proportion of people do what they are told to do," he wrote, "irrespective of the content of the act and without limitations of conscience, so long as they perceive that the command comes from a legitimate authority."[*]

Evangelical Christianity has at least claimed to hold to the Reformation principle of *sola Scriptura*, which is not, and never was, the claim that Scripture is the only *authority* of any kind. Scripture itself speaks of the authority of parents, of governments, of the church, even of the revelation embedded in the creation itself. The

---

[*]Stanley Milgram, *Obedience to Authority: An Experimental View* (New York: Harper & Row, 1974), 228–29.

claim is instead that Scripture is the *final* authority, the norm that norms all other norms. Jesus honors the authority of his parents (Luke 2:51) but was more than willing at points to appeal to a higher authority and thus not to do what they wished (Luke 2:49; John 2:4). Jesus honors the religious authorities of the priesthood and the temple (Matt. 23:1–3), but he is also more than willing to defy these authorities (Matt. 21:23–27). Jesus is willing to give Caesar his coin when taxed (Mark 12:17), but is not willing to give Pilate his voice when commanded (Matt. 27:11–14).

Jesus, though, maintains the ultimate authority of the Scriptures, which he identifies with the Word of God himself (Mark 12:35– 37). Even when in the Sermon on the Mount Jesus seems to be at odds with the Law of Moses, our Lord is quick to say that he is teaching an intensification, not a contradiction, of the Scripture, which he holds to be true and authoritative even in its minutest details (Matt. 5:17–20). The Scripture, Jesus tells us, "cannot be broken" (John 10:35). The same principle is at work with Jesus' apostles, inspired by his Spirit. Paul, for example, pens entire letters showing how the inclusion of the Gentiles and the passing away of circumcision are taught ahead of time in the Old Testament Scriptures (Rom. 4:1–28; Gal. 3:1–29). Paul is willing to defy even the authority of an apostle (Gal. 2:11–14), but is not willing to defy Scripture. Peter himself, though willing to argue with Paul personally, is not willing to defy the inspired Scripture written through Paul (2 Pet. 3:14–16).

The claim, "The Bible says . . ." can remind us that every other claimed authority is accountable to a truth outside of itself. The church, and even the apostles themselves, have a derivative authority. Jesus can rebuke his disciples, even the closest to him (the examples with Peter are too numerous to recite here), but not the other way around. And Scripture, Old and New Testaments, claims to be the voice of Jesus speaking (1 Pet. 1:10–11). The church has legitimate authority. When the church rightly discerns a moral failing, and speaks to it rightly, this word is that of Jesus himself (Matt. 18:20; 1 Cor. 5:3–4). But the church can and does err—and can even lose the lampstand of Christ's presence through disobedience or through false teaching (Rev. 2:5). How do we determine whether a church is exercising authority, or refusing to exercise authority, in a way that is out of step with God's purpose? We do what the apostles taught us to do: we judge the church by what has been revealed in Scripture, not the other way around (Acts 17:11; 2 Tim. 3:1–5). The psalms of David and the proverbs of Solomon are authoritative over us, but not because David and Solomon held the office of king. David also said, "Go get Bathsheba," and Solomon also said, "What harm can a few idol-worshipping high places do?" The authority of David and Solomon over us comes when God is speaking through them. How has the church recognized Scripture as Scripture? The testimony of the Holy Spirit, working through the church. "My sheep hear my voice . . . and they follow me," Jesus tells us (John 10:27).

Does this mean that every individual sheep recognizes the voice of Christ speaking in the Scriptures? No. Simon Peter didn't understand the cross, at first. Paul and Barnabas disagreed over whether

Mark could be trusted (Acts 15:36–39). Martin Luther didn't like the book of James. Our heroes and heroines in church history have gotten things wrong, doctrinally and morally. Parts of the church were wrong—satanically wrong—on issues of righteousness and justice, such as the Spanish Inquisition and the scourge of human slavery. Over the long run, though, the people of God recognize the Scriptures, not because the church creates the Scriptures but because the Scriptures create the church. A final authority for Scripture means that every human authority and institution is accountable to a truth outside of its own making. When any tribe or individual or government or political party or politician or pastor or church demands the ability to define what is real and what is unreal, what is true and what is false, step back and ask if this person or institution is trying to become your god.

Inhabit the Bible. That's a Sunday school answer, but it's because Sunday school was right. Evangelical Christians are thought to be a people of the Bible. And with good reason: we are, after all, the ones who pioneered Sunday schools to teach the next generation the Bible, who expend massive resources on Bible translation for people around the world, who exhort one another to personal daily Bible reading. David Nienhuis, a professor of biblical studies, however, writes about how his students struggle with the biblical material "because they have been trained to be Bible *quoters*, not Bible *readers*." He writes: "They have the capacity to recall a relevant biblical text in support of a particular doctrinal point, or in opposition to a hot spot in the cultural wars, or in hope of emotional support when times get tough. They approach the Bible as a sort of reference book, a collection of useful God-quotes that can be looked up as one would locate a word in a dictionary or an entry in an encyclopedia."*

Some evangelical Christians know Scripture in order to debate predestination or women's ordination—in the same way the pragmatic Christians they despise know how to use Scripture to address melancholy on the job or endurance through toilet training a child—and yet don't know the difference between Josiah and Jehoiakim. It seems to them to be beside the point. This is a bigger problem than whether a politician knows how to say "Second Corinthians" rather than "Two Corinthians" when seeking votes at an evangelical confab. This is not biblical illiteracy, but what Neil Postman warned us would be more dangerous than illiteracy—"aliteracy." The "aliterate," Postman argued, is the person who can read but doesn't.† The Bible, however, works in a different way than by distilling it into abstractions—whether theological syllogisms or practical life tips or worldview axioms.

The authority of Scripture works itself out in a human life not like a "worldview" mapping out exhaustive responses to the controversies in which one is already engaged, but first by submerging a

---

*David R. Nienhuis, *A Concise Guide to Reading the New Testament: A Canonical Introduction* (Grand Rapids: Baker, 2018), 2–4.

†Neil Postman, *Conscientious Objections: Stirring Up Trouble About Language, Technology, and Education* (New York: Random House, 1988), 111.

---

life in a different storyline altogether. A renewed experience of biblical authority can illuminate what's at the heart of every claim to authority in any community: a storyline that makes sense of the meaning of one's world and one's place in it. We can see the awful ways such stories can work in, for instance, the *volk* mythology of Nazi-era Germany or in the use of "blood-and-soil" mythology today. Those stories are always most powerful when they are assumed and not questioned. The Bible proposes an alternative storyline—a true storyline—that invites the community and the individual to find themselves in an already-existing story—the ongoing life of Christ. When Jesus was tempted by the devil in the wilderness, he responded with Scripture. But Jesus' response was not just proof texts against false teaching. By citing the particular Scriptures he did, from Deuteronomy, Jesus was pointing to the fact that he knew what the devil was up to—because the people of God had already been in the place of testing—to seek food, protection, and glory from somewhere other than from God. The people of God had failed in the wilderness before; the Son of God would not. That calls us to ask of every authority, "What story are they telling me about themselves? About me?" and how does it relate to what's been revealed to me: "I am the Lord your God who brought you out of Egypt" and "You are crucified with Christ to walk in newness of life."

Evangelical Christianity's emphasis on the Bible is part of the sense of the personal. The Bible is not just the territory of the church but of each individual Christian—with personal daily devotionals, or "quiet times," expected for personal growth in Christ. At times, this personal emphasis—as with conversion—has gone too far. See, for instance, the proliferation of "study Bibles" marketed around demographic generations or even occupations or around the often ghostwritten "study notes" of evangelical celebrities. The sense that the Bible can speak personally has led to such extremes at times as Christians flipping open a Bible and pointing randomly at a verse to see what God was saying about a particular decision or life inflection point, much in the way a stack of tarot cards might work. The devotional aspects of Bible reading have sometimes eclipsed any depth of contemplation of the text, much less the reading the church has had of that text over the centuries. And yet, however skewed and exaggerated, the basic sense of the Bible as both a personal need and as a personal address—"Jesus loves me, this I know, for the Bible tells me so . . ."—gets at something important at the heart of the biblical claim about itself and about the hunger of a depersonalized and lonely age. The Bible reshapes a sense of authority by re-forming not just the intellect but the affections and the imagination too. This works in a subterranean way— like, as Jesus would put it, yeast working invisibly through a loaf of bread. That's because the most important ways that we are changed are most often invisible to us.

Shortly after the January 6 insurrection, a Christian radio show interviewed me about it, taking calls from listeners. One seemed ambivalent about the attack on the Capitol, wondering, if she had been there, how this was the wrong thing to do. I agreed that there were many difficult ethical questions with which to grapple and for which we might never come to conclusive answers, but that this wasn't one of them. "If you see someone building a gallows, no matter where you are, leave," I said. A biblically literate Christianity will not so much have guidebooks and policy papers but a people who know a story well enough to recognize when someone is attempting to use us, to fly a gospel message over a gallows, to use a church youth group to groom a child toward rape, to baptize a political movement to the point that "I alone can fix it" sounds like "Thus saith the Lord." And yet, it cannot be enough for us to recognize wrong use of authority. You must come to love the voice of Christ, handed down through the ages in the Word of God, enough to be able to sing, once again, "We have heard the joyful sound—Jesus saves."

CHAPTER THREE

LOSING OUR IDENTITY

How Conversion Can Save Us from Culture Wars

T he woman looked at the ground as she asked us to pray for her daughter. Several of us were in a circle around her, and she fought tears as she told us how much it hurt to see her child walk away from what they'd taught her. I was expecting her to give the typical story of a young person who, out on her own for the first time, starts to question the faith she has learned. Maybe the daughter was an atheist now, or dabbling in an Eastern religion. But that wasn't right, because a few moments later, the mother mentioned how her daughter was a Christian and attended church every Sunday. My mind then expected to hear about a double life— Saturday night at the club, Sunday morning in the pew. Or maybe the daughter had moved in with her boyfriend or was pregnant and unmarried. But, no, the presenting issue wasn't any of those things, the mother said, it was a bumper sticker on the daughter's car when she pulled into the driveway for the family's Thanksgiving gathering.

"No one said anything about it," the mother said. "She didn't even mention it, but we all felt the tension." Once again my mind was racing ahead of the storyline, expecting to hear that the bumper sticker read, "My Other Car Is a Broom: Celebrate Wicca" or "Pass Joints, Not Judgment: Legalize Marijuana" or maybe even one of the Coexist stickers with all the symbols of each world religion bunched together in the word. None of that was the case either. The bumper sticker read, "Any Sane, Functioning Adult for President, 2020."

I must have visibly grimaced. I don't mind praying for anybody— and not just for so-called "big" things. But still. "Really?" I thought. First of all, how is it that we've arrived at the place where when one sees the words *sane* and *functioning*, one immediately concludes, "That means she's not supporting our candidate"? More importantly, who cares if she doesn't support your candidate? Is that really what it means to reject the values her family taught her? I decided what God was asking of me in that situation was to set my irritation aside and to pray for her. "Don't focus on the situation," I told myself. "Focus on her pain. I can pray for that." This mother-daughter tension was more dramatic but not all that different from a scenario I've heard of and seen at countless Thanksgiving tables, church potlucks, and even around the coffeepot at the prayer breakfast.

Long ago, in what seems like another lifetime, I would often say to churches, "Elections make Christians go crazy." What I defined as "crazy" in the before-times now seems as calm and innocent as a neighborhood food drive by comparison. Not long ago, I sat with a group of burned-out, discouraged pastors and one of them asked, "What was it about 2021, that year specifically, that broke so many of us?" I had no answer until another pastor replied that it was because anyone can endure almost anything if one knows an end is in sight. People assumed that the craziness would dissipate after the 2016 election. Then they assumed it would go away after the country adjusted to having a president like we'd never seen before. Some people expected that once things "went back to boring," say, with the election of Joe Biden, that that would do it. People would move on. Some people fantasized that a big national emergency— a September 11 or a Pearl Harbor—would unite the country and things would be back as they should be. Then came a big national emergency—a global pandemic—and things became crazier, not saner. Yes, election years are always a bit fraught, but we usually have an endpoint to them. In this moment in America, it seems that, with apologies to the psalmist and to the apostle Peter, a thousand years is as an election day and an election day is as a thousand years. Within the church, this tension feels especially pointed and exhausting. The question I keep getting from Christians is, "Why does everyone, everywhere, seem to have decided to have a nervous breakdown, all at the same time?"

That's a good question. Every time I talk to an older expert, especially in history or psychology, I will always ask, "Is everything really uniquely crazy right now or is this just life, and I never knew it?" Some of it is, of course, the way life always is—with nothing new under the sun—but a great deal of it is new to what we've ever experienced in our lifetime. Political scientist Christopher Freiman explains it as the "monopolization of our identity by politics."* In our time, he argues, politics is rarely about how we cooperate to solve civic problems and is more about the expression of one's entire identity. Politics now is about whether you prefer Walmart Supercenters or Whole Foods Markets, whether you prefer stock-car racing or soccer, whether you drive a clean-energy electric vehicle or a pickup truck, and so on. This, he notes, is exhausting. It's exhausting to define ourselves not by who and what we love but by who and what we hate. And these partisan identities, he notes, "are increasingly anchored to hatred of the out-party rather than affection for the in-party." Freiman writes, "We hate the other team more than we like our team. Why? We need to ramp up our animosity to the out-party to rationalize our continued dedication to our own party despite its obvious shortcomings. ('I know my party can be spineless and ineffective but I've got to stick with them because the other side is downright evil.')."† That's why not just every election but every political conversation is so often posed in apocalyptic terms of existential threat.

What it takes to be a "real conservative" or a "real progressive" tomorrow is often the opposite of what it is today. And to be part of

---

*Christopher Freiman, *Why It's OK to Ignore Politics* (New York: Routledge, 2021), 122.

†Ibid., 123.

one's tribe, one must not have questioned loyalties. This sort of identity protection leads to the kind of constant vigilance that is exhausting. It leads, ultimately, not to the development of civic engagement and coherent political philosophies, but to the reverse—to the sort of "burned over districts" that would be left in the wake of religious "revivals" that were defined not by the gospel and the ordinary patterns of sanctification but by endless enthusiasms and spectacular experiences of ecstasy. Freiman writes that part of the reason politics has swallowed everything is that we have fewer and fewer of what he calls "cross-cutters" in American life. He defines this "cross-cutting" sort of identity as "people whose partisan identities do *not* align with their other social identities in the standard pattern (picture a Prius-driving Unitarian Republican who regularly attends vegan cooking classes)." Because these people have their identities not all bound up in one temporal thing or another, he argues, they are "less hostile to out-party members and less likely to get angry about politics. But as these 'cross-cutters' grow scarce, politics gets bloodier."* When religious identity is added to the mix, the stakes grow even higher.

Political movements—especially authoritarian and totalitarian ones—almost always want to co-opt religion. Sometimes that takes the form of a Nebuchadnezzar building a golden statue of himself, but, more often, it takes the form of these movements seeking to claim already-existing religions for themselves. Caesar created an

---

*Freiman, *Why It's OK to Ignore Politics*, 123.

---

imperial cult for himself by joining it to the already-existing worship of the Roman pantheon. The Chinese Communist Party does this with Confucianism, the ayatollahs with Islam, and the examples could go on and on. As one group of scholars has noted, "Religious identity is about belonging, not necessarily believing."* That's true—and throughout most societies in history one need not have sorted out "What religion am I?" If one is born in Saudi Arabia, one would be Muslim; in certain parts of India, then Hindu; in Ireland, then Catholic; in Greece, then Eastern Orthodox; and so on.

Something darker than just that is emerging, or reemerging, though. Researcher Tobias Cremer has examined this in a range of contexts—from Hungarian to Dutch to German to North American populist movements—and concludes that the "benefits of such a pact are obvious" because the "coalition has conservative Christians as junior partners, who provide a powerful financial and electoral resource, and a convenient fig-leaf for respectability." Cremer notes that one can find crosses and Crusader imagery and (in France) Joan of Arc statues—often held aloft by those who are atheists or agnostics or otherwise unchurched. Why? According to Cremer, they represent an "extreme form of a secularized Christianity" in which these concepts are symbols of an imagined "white and masculine past." Think again of the Jesus Saves sign and other

---

*David M. Elcott, et al., *Faith, Nationalism, and the Future of Liberal Democracy* (South Bend: University of Notre Dame Press, 2021), 23.

Christian symbols at the January 6, 2021, attack on the Capitol. Cremer would argue that this is not as unusual as it seems. Conservative Christian symbols, images, or memes are quite commonly seen throughout both Europe and North America right along with iconography from such past "Lost Causes" as the Vikings or the Confederacy. This is because, he notes, what passes for Christianity in this context "is little more than an ethno-cultural identifier that is increasingly dissociated from Christian theological beliefs, Christian private ethics, or Christian institutions like the church."* This is not only true of the more "organized" aspects of these forms of Christian nationalism, but often also of the "lone wolves" radicalized by such viewpoints from a distance. The domestic terrorist who massacred African American shoppers in a Buffalo, New York, grocery store posted a manifesto in which he discussed his influences and ideology, including much about "white genocide" and the "Great Replacement Theory." When addressing whether he is a Christian, the killer said that he was not by the definition of believing by faith for salvation or of confessing sins to God or of believing there to be an afterlife. He held, though, he wrote, to "Christian values," defined as Western civilization and white identity. To whatever followers he might have, the killer wrote that they "don't need to have a personal relationship with God or Jesus to fight for our

---

*Tobias Cremer, "The Capitol Storming Epitomizes the Shift from a Religious to a Post-Religious Right," *Providence*, January 27, 2021.

Christian cultural heritage."* One European scholar notes French Identitarians organizing get-togethers in the streets to indulge in pork sausages and red wine in front of their Muslim and Jewish neighbors—to make the point of who the "other" is and to mock those who are not one of them. "The sausages and red wine are essentially caricatures of the Eucharist, metaphors that destroy what is being mimicked, in other words the Christianity that they supposedly promote."† What the "elements" in such a ceremony convey is not the body of Christ broken for the world, the blood of Christ poured out for all, but "This is us." One observer noted that in the United States the prototype of the sort of Christian culture-warrior is one who "would rather be the lone Christian in a neighborhood of atheists who put up Christmas trees for cultural reasons than the only white person in a neighborhood of Senegalese Christians."‡

Scholar Matthew Rose has argued that, around the world, "a post-Christian right is struggling to be born."§ Unlike what we typically think of as "conservatism" in the setting of a liberal democracy, this post-Christian right, he contends, will seek to give "defiant ex-

---

*Jeet Heer, "Christianity's Postliberal Critics," *Commonweal*, July/August 2022, 64.

†Olivier Roy, *Is Europe Christian?*, trans. Cynthia Schoch (New York: Oxford University Press, 153–54.

‡Benjamin Dueholm, "Who's a Persecuted Christian?," *Christian Century*, February 24, 2021, 39.

§Matthew Rose, *The World After Liberalism: Five Thinkers Who Inspired the Radical Right* (New Haven: Yale University Press, 2021), 146.

---

pression to primordial passions, once disciplined by religion, that liberalism tried to repress—about preserving cultural differences, punishing enemies, and deposing disloyal elites."* Rose warns: "But should a post-Christian right seek unity in what binds human beings from below, rather than what unites them from above, a decisive step will have been taken. It will represent an attempt to undo the Christian revolution by severing the connection between Western culture and transcendence."† But he also notes that there is more than one way to reject the objectionable aspects of Christianity. One way is to replace Christianity with some form of paganism, which many of these thinkers wish to do, and another is to paganize Christianity. Rather than rejecting Christianity, he argues, this movement could "clothe itself in Christianity, claiming a religious defense of ethnic or cultural identity."‡ In other words, the step before replacing Jesus with Thor is to turn Jesus into Thor. The contrast of paganism or semi-paganism with the Christian gospel is the far less dangerous of the two options. If all that were at stake were democracy and global stability, these would be critically important issues. But for evangelical Christians, the stakes are not just those but what we mean when we say "Christianity" in the first place.

Christian nationalism is the use of Christian words, symbols, or

*Ibid.

†Ibid., 146–47.

‡Ibid., 147.

rituals as a means to the end of shoring up an ethnic or a national identity. At first, some conservative Christians dismissed the very existence of Christian nationalism, arguing that it was a creation of the Left to keep religious people out of the public square. Gradually, though, some of these leaders started claiming the name for themselves proudly. And some have attempted to do both at more or less the same time. To be sure, there is a secular Left that does not understand religion and would see almost any expression of it, at least on the side of orthodoxy, as a threat. These are the type of people who, if given an audience with the pope, would expect him to start the meeting by identifying his pronouns. Nonetheless, Christian nationalism is not only real, but it increasingly is interconnected with movements all around the world. Perhaps the key component of Christian nationalism might ironically enough be defined by a Jewish thinker, increasingly applauded by American evangelical audiences, Yoram Hazony, who argues, "Where there is a large Christian majority, the public life of the country has to be Christian," since "where there's a majority of a certain culture, they get the public culture."* That makes sense in a context in which religion is an external reality—enforced in terms of certain rituals and practices, or by virtue of one's birth or national solidarity or biological kinship or racial identity.

---

*Cited in William A. Galston, "Whose Good, Anyway," *American Purpose*, January 21, 2021.

But is that Christianity?

A man from a much more formal, liturgical tradition than mine complained to me once that evangelical Christians were giving up on blood. For years, he said, he slipped into evangelical Christian church services from time to time, "Just to hear people who weren't ashamed of the blood of Christ." His parish, he assured me, believed not just in the blood of Jesus but in its real presence in the Eucharist, but he said it was considered too gauche there to talk about it in the visceral—and to some, disturbing—ways that evangelical Christians do—with all our songs about "power in the blood" and being "washed in the blood." Even so, he said, he was finding fewer and fewer churches—even very conservative evangelical churches—that still talked and sang that way, with the blood drained out into bloodless abstractions or practicalities. Many of them probably started downplaying the blood talk, he speculated, because they wanted to draw in people in their communities, people for whom the blood language, if taken too far, might sound, at best, low-class and unsophisticated and, at worst, cultlike. He stopped going to the successful suburban churches, and began searching out gospel rescue missions for the poor and Christian recovery programs for the addicted. With the hurting and the powerless, he said, there's where one still heard about blood, about "power, power, wonder-working power, in the blood of the Lamb." He said, "I know you all want to reach people—but, it seems to me, when you're choosing between comfort and blood, too many of you are making the wrong choice. Once you've given up the blood, you've given up everything."

Indeed you have.

This conversation comes to mind often when I consider what is sometimes called "Christian nationalism"—either in its more common and less virulent strain of "God and country" politicized civil religion or in the much more explicit and terrifying ways that we have seen Christian symbols co-opted by demagogic and authoritarian ethnocentric or nationalist movements in Europe and Latin America and even in the hands of January 6 insurrectionists in the United States. What we are bargaining away, in mild or severe cases of these nationalistic movements, is the blood of Christ for blood-and-soil, and that is not an even trade. The gospel according to Jesus is not an external affirmation of generic belief, from a heart still untransformed. The gospel according to Jesus is not accepting Christianity as a ticket of admission into society. The gospel according to Jesus means that there is one God and one mediator between God and men, the man Christ Jesus (1 Tim. 2:5). One can stand before God at judgment only by union with the crucified and resurrected Jesus Christ. And can only come into union with Christ through faith (Rom. 3:21–31).

That faith—as defined by Jesus and his apostles—does not come through the proxy of a nation or a ruler or even a religious structure. If that were the case, then John the Baptist would not have needed to preach repentance to the descendants of Abraham (Matt. 3: 9–10). And if that were the case, the apostle Paul could have found no fault in those who served the false gods chosen for them by their national or family traditions (Acts 17:22–31). Instead, the gospel addresses each person—one by one—as one who will stand at the Judgment Seat, who will give an account, and who is commanded to personally believe the gospel and repent of sin (Rom. 10:9–17). As Jesus said to Nicodemus by night: "Truly, truly, I say to you, unless one is born again he cannot see the kingdom of God" (John 3:3). And how does this new birth, this personal receiving of Christ by faith, happen? It does not happen by the changing of a family crest or by a vote of the city council. It happens through the Spirit opening the heart, through the "open statement of the truth" commending itself to each conscience (2 Cor. 4:2).

Christian nationalism is not a politically enthusiastic version of Christianity, nor is it a religiously informed patriotism. Christian nationalism is a prosperity gospel for nation-states, a liberation theology for white people. In that it has more in common with the lifeless establishments, the old liberalisms, and some of the social gospels, which preferred a gospel that changed externals and did not demand personal repentance and faith. It submerges personal transformation under social transformation, thus making both impossible. As Russell Kirk once explained about the impersonal viewpoint of the collectivist: "He cannot see the trees for the forest."* According to the almost-gospels we've seen periodically

---

*Russell Kirk, *Concise Guide to Conservatism* (Washington, DC: Regnery, 1957, 2019), 73.

throughout history, as long as one's country was "Christian," then one was a Christian too. As long as one's ruler was "Christian," then one was a part of the church. As long as one's morality was adequately regulated, whether by law or by social custom, then one was a good Christian. That's all well and good—unless there's a hell. If Jesus is telling the truth that there is a judgment to come, and if Jesus is telling the truth that no one comes to the Father except through him (John 14:6), and if Jesus is telling the truth that "coming to him" means not just external behavior but faith in him, then no legal edict or social pressure can regenerate a human heart. Such things cannot make a person into a Christian, only into a pretend Christian. External conformity can make a person into a follower of Baal or Asherah or Dagon or a thousand other deities. That is not the gospel of Jesus Christ. Jesus taught us that nothing coming in from the outside can defile a person, but rather what is within the heart of a person that defiles him (Mark 7:14–23).

Of the blood-and-soil impulses of such movements as Christian nationalism we must ask what's underneath? As the sociologist Peter Berger noted about the human motives for the kind of collectivism we see here and elsewhere: "The entire collectivity, bound together by ties of blood, thus becomes (to its own self-understanding) quite concretely immortal, for it carried with it through time the *same* fundamental life that is incarnate in each of its members." They are seeking a canopy of protection—from death, from shame, from guilt, from humiliation—in the group.* The quest is for everlasting life—a life seen in the ongoing life of the tribe, not the person. This is precisely the mindset John the Baptist bulldozed when he said, on the banks of the Jordan: "And do not begin to say to yourselves, 'We have Abraham as our father.' For I tell you, God is able from these stones to raise up children for Abraham" (Luke 3:8). The question is the same as it always was, "Teacher, what shall I do to inherit eternal life?" And when told to love God and neighbor, the rejoinder is as it often is, "And who is my neighbor?" (Luke 10:25, 29). Just as in Jesus' inaugural sermon, the message of freedom, liberation, and anointing is received with jubilation, as long as it is thought to apply to the already-existing national or ethnic or kinship categories, but when told that the ways of God reach beyond all that, to the Gentile widow and the Syrian soldier, the jubilation gives way to rage (Luke 4:16–30).

This is not a new drive. Jesus was well aware of the pull of humanity to a gospel that is about finding a political avatar or accommodating the appetites. When Jesus perceived the crowds were coming to make him king, he walked away (John 6:15). And when the crowds assembled to hear him after his multiplication of bread and fish, he told them "you are seeking me, not because you saw signs, but because you ate your fill of the loaves" (John 6:26). He was

---

*Peter Berger, *The Sacred Canopy: Elements of a Sociological Theory of Religion* (New York: Anchor, 1967), 62–63.

willing to see those crowds walk away—and his own disciples tempted to do so (John 6:60–61)—because what they would have received would have been the fulfillment of populist fervor, but it wouldn't have been him.

But what happens when the sound of the wind seems to merely be a white-noise recording? What happens when the motivations of supposedly born-again people seem to be lined up exactly with their tribal boundaries or their base appetites, in a way that would be the same even if Jesus were still dead? Christian nationalisms and civil religions are a kind of Great Commission in reverse, in which the nations seek to make disciples of themselves, using the authority of Jesus to baptize their national identity in the name of the blood and of the soil and of the political order. The gospel is not a means to any end, except for the end of union with the crucified and resurrected Christ who transcends, and stands in judgment over, every group, every identity, every nationality, every culture. Christian nationalism might well "work" in the short term in cementing bonds of cultural solidarity according the flesh. But apart from the shedding of blood there can be no forgiveness of sins. Apart from the Holy Spirit, there can be no newness of life. Christian nationalism cannot turn back secularism, because it is just another form of it. In fact, it is an even more virulent form of secularism because it pronounces as "Christian" what cannot stand before the Judgment Seat of Christ. Christian nationalism cannot save the world; it cannot even save *you*.

And yet, in a world in which everything is politics, everything is a culture war, everything is identity protection, religion becomes a useful tool to take all that and make it seem transcendent. When a religion is seen as a political agenda in search of a gospel useful enough to accommodate it, one will end up pleasing those who see the primacy of the politics while losing those who believe the gospel. In many ways, the politicized evangelicalism we see everywhere around us is to actual Christianity what the Nation of Islam is to the actual Muslim faith. Both are nationalistic vehicles of identity politics, needing a transcendent creed on which to ride. Culture-warring is easier than conversion because, as George Orwell once wrote of "transferred nationalism," it "is a way of attaining salvation without altering one's conduct."* The stakes are much higher, though, if the Christian religion is actually *true*. As Lesslie Newbigin warned: "The confusion of a particular and fallible set of political and oral judgments with the cause of Jesus Christ is more dangerous than the open rejection of the claim of Christ in Islam, just as the shrine of Jeroboam at Bethel was more dangerous to the faith of Israel than was the open paganism of her neighbors, for the worship of Baal was being carried on under the name of Yahweh."†

In some ways, American evangelical Christianity should have seen this posture coming, since we test-drove it first. James Dav-

---

*George Orwell, "Notes on Nationalism," in *Essays: Everyman's Library*, ed. John Carey (New York: Knopf, 2002), 872.

†Lesslie Newbigin, *Foolishness to the Greeks: The Gospel and Western Culture* (Grand Rapids: Eerdmans, 1986), 116–17.

ison Hunter warned over a decade ago that much of American evangelical "culture war" engagement was based in a heightened sense of resentment, which he defined as a combination of anger, envy, hate, rage, and revenge, in which a sense of injury and anxiety become key to the group's identity. Often, this sort of rage mixed with anxiety is bound up not so much with a fear of specific policy outcomes but as a fear more primal, more akin to middle school: the fear of humiliation. What Donald Trump said about foreign countries vis-à-vis the United States could also be thought of as elite culture vis-à-vis American evangelicals: "They are laughing at us." Anyone who has worked with or lived with a severely narcissistic personality can testify that one of the most dangerous times for an eruption of temper—whether of the "hot" kind of rage or the "cool" kind of manipulation—comes when the person feels himself or herself to be humiliated. Why? This is because, when self is at the center, humiliation *feels* like an existential threat. It feels like a kind of death, and the kind of death that leaves one exposed and ridiculed by the outside world.

In Hunter's view, a resentment posture is heightened when the group holds a sense of entitlement—to greater respect, to greater power, to a place of majority status. This posture, he warned, is a political psychology that expresses itself with "the condemnation and denigration of enemies in the effort to subjugate and dominate those who are culpable." Not for nothing did Jerry Falwell Sr. name his political movement a "moral majority"—the idea being that, hearkening back to Richard Nixon's "silent majority," most

Americans wanted the same "values" as conservative evangelicals; it was just that they were stymied by coastal liberal elites who were able to overrule the wishes of most people. Often, whether of immigrant caravans overwhelming the border or the concept of a global pandemic being developed by American elites to control the population with vaccines to the rhetoric of Satan-worshipping pedophile rings at the highest levels of government, much of the most contentious aspects of American life are about the question, "Who is trying to take America away from us?" Amanda Ripley, in her study on conflict, found that humiliation happens whenever our brains have conducted "a rapid-fire evaluation of events and fit it into our understanding of the world." But that's not enough. She argues, "To be brought low, we have to first see ourselves as belonging up high." She gives the trivial example of her once-ever golfing outing, in which she missed the ball over and over again. She laughed at herself, she said, but she didn't feel humiliated. That's because, she writes, being good at golf is not part of her identity. If Tiger Woods—renowned to be the best golfer in the world—performed the same way, it would feel humiliating, especially on camera before an entire watching world.*

In order to understand this sort of resentment, one must start by rightly identifying its origin. Some would suggest that the grievances were specifically theological or ideological—and yet survey after

---

*Amanda Ripley, *High Conflict: Why We Get Trapped and How We Get Out* (New York: Simon & Schuster, 2021), 125.

survey show that the issues assumed to be of most importance to evangelical Christian culture-warriors—abortion or marriage, for instance—are of much lower priority than issues that are far more "secular" and yet far more emotionally visceral: namely, immigration and race. Even concerns over religious liberty are hardly ever articulated at the popular level in terms of genuine threats to the freedom of religious believers, say, the status of the Religious Freedom Restoration Act or possible accreditation or public funding threats to traditionalist religious colleges, universities, or charities. Instead, they are more often framed in terms of illusory threats— such as the supposed loss of the greeting "Merry Christmas" in stores—that are not about freedom in a pluralizing society but instead about an identity politics resentment at a perceived loss of acknowledgment and respect from the outside world. Research also leads away from the idea that the eruption of "backlash" we've seen in recent years is caused by job losses in rural or Rust Belt America due to economic globalization.

In an exhaustive study of the background of those participating in the January 6 insurrection at the United States Capitol, *The Atlantic*'s Barton Gellman demonstrates that the predictor for whether someone would be more or less likely to participate in this act of violence was not "economic anxiety" (participants were disproportionately well-off) or whether they lived in "Red states" or "Blue states." The only factor that accurately predicted likelihood of such violence was whether they lived in a county where the white population was going down or up.* The sense of vulnerability and threat here must then be amplified with a mythology that explains *why* white evangelical Christianity represents the *real* America. This is how a market is created for the easily debunked idea that the American founders were evangelical Christians. The idea provides for both a secularized Eden and a secularized Fall, for both the entitlement and the outrage, enabling evangelical Christians to feel *both* like a dominant majority *and* a beleaguered minority, *at the same time.*

This combination of nostalgia and resentment, of power and of powerlessness, is easily manipulated once manufactured. In analyzing aspects of "high conflict" in any institution or community, Amanda Ripley argues that a key step is to identify who are the "conflict entrepreneurs" in that orbit. "Notice who delights in each new plot twist of a feud," she writes. "Who is quick to validate every lament and to articulate wrongs no one has even thought of?"† In this era of evangelical Christianity, such "conflict entrepreneurs" might be talk-radio hosts seeking an audience, social media combatants seeking followers, or politicians seeking a base. One observer of demagogic movements notes that a key for demagogues is to create the sort of nostalgia that creates a "pain of defeat," which then produces "a feeling of victimhood through which national

---

*Barton Gellman, "January 6 Was Practice," *The Atlantic*, January 2022.
†Ripley, *High Conflict*, 114.

cohesion starts to emerge." He notes, "The paradoxical effect of re- sentment is to convert power into a feeling of powerlessness, and vice versa."* That sort of powerlessness leads a people who feel this way to seek the kind of leaders who can fight off the enemies who have overrun their inheritance, who have humiliated them, and who threaten to take their children away. In such a context, felt vulnerability leads to a contempt for vulnerability in others. How different this is from the One who told us that no one took his life; he laid it down and would pick it up again (John 10:17–18). Resent- ment is the way of Cain—who simmered in rage at his brother because Cain's sacrifice was not recognized by God and Abel's was.

The way of the cross is the way of Abel—who offered his sacri- fice even to the giving up of his own life. Some would say, I suppose, "See, that's the problem! Abel ended up dead! Cain at least was a fighter!" That makes sense from one point of view. The problem is that that point of view is at war with that of the Bible, which says: "By faith Abel offered to God a more acceptable sacrifice than Cain, through which he was commended as righteous, God com- mending him by accepting his gifts. And through his faith, though he died, he still speaks" (Heb. 11:4). Indeed, the Bible defines the gospel itself in terms of the blood of Christ "that speaks a better word than the blood of Abel" and warns, "See that you do not re- fuse him who is speaking" (Heb. 12:24–25).

---

*William Davies, *Nervous States: Democracy and the Decline of Reason* (New York: W. W. Norton, 2018), 145.

So what should you do to hold fast to the kind of conversionism that can counteract the ever-heightening culture-warring and ever-expanding political idolatries of the moment?

Refuse to Secularize. If you've long been in an evangelical environment, you probably were warned often to, as Paul told Timothy, "Watch your life and doctrine closely" (1 Tim. 4:16 NIV). Maybe you were already attentive to the ways that you could be tempted to be "tossed to and fro . . . carried about by every wind of doctrine" (Eph. 4:14). Maybe you assumed, though, that this could happen just by a leftward move, by subtracting the supernatural or the more difficult moral mandates of the Christian faith in such a way that you could whittle yourself down to atheism. Be careful to note that there is more than one way for you to secularize, and in one of those ways your atheism can make you feel even *more* Christian than you did before; all it takes is substituting adrenaline for the Holy Spirit, political "awakening" for rebirth, quarrelsomeness for sanctification, and a visible tribal identity for the kingdom of God.

Years ago, the great controversy in Christian circles was how to respond to the "New Atheist" movements of Christopher Hitchens, Richard Dawkins, and others. These seemed especially perilous not because they were persuading many people with their arguments but because they were able to "troll" Christians by ridiculing and mocking our beliefs in media-savvy and quotable ways. One atheist, though not nearly as well known, wrote that the New Atheist strategy was all wrong. The argument shouldn't be framed, he wrote, around why theism is wrong, but where it is treated as "irrelevant and beneath serious consideration." He wrote: "We should aim to get to where belief in God and faith-based thinking are considered so obsolete that they bear no relevance on the functioning of our societies and academies." Don't attack religion straight on, he argued, though it must be uprooted. Getting to the "post-faith society" this atheist wants would require an effort to "delegitimize faith." Religious people can start to see belief in God and faith in Christ as "so obsolete that they bear no relevance on the functioning of our societies and our academies." The way that's done is not by arguing theism versus atheism with Christians, he wrote, but by "helping people uproot their reliance on faith, securing secular societies creating and consuming educational materials in the right subjects, modifying our thinking and our behavior to match, and *finding ways to fill the needs currently filled by religion*" (emphasis mine).*

Within just a few years, this atheist found support with a "Christian activist" who ran cruises for Christian ministries. This atheist soon was appearing on "documentaries" and invited to speak at Christian pastors' conferences and on Christian media, to attack as "cultural Marxists" Christians concerned about racial injustice or who called for reforms to deal with sexual abuse. The atheist had not changed his mind on God, was not a new Christian wanting to combat the error of his old ways. The atheist, though, was able to tap into a market of professing Christians who were willing to see

---

*James Lindsay, *Everybody Is Wrong About God* (Durham: Pitchstone, 2015), 25–28.

"Christianity" as fundamentally an ethnic or national or political category, and "heresy" as whatever deviates from that. Who needs to talk anyone out of belief in God or faith in Christ when all one needs to do is to get them to see those things as irrelevant to what "really matters"? One need not lead people to check a box that they are atheists. They can still be Christians, as long as they are motivated by questions other than those of the judgment of God and the gospel of Christ. One can get all the benefits of a religion in which theism is beneath serious consideration, all the while transferring the zeal that comes with Christianity to other, more temporal, more "important" concerns. One can secularize Christians thoroughly, without them ever even seeing it themselves. And in this sort of post-truth era, very few people are going to wonder how it's not a self-contradiction for Christian nationalists to use the testimony of atheists to attack historic gospel Christians for abandoning the "sufficiency of Scripture." After all, who is going to cite the Scripture that "the fool says in his heart 'There is no God'" (Ps. 14:1) when there are so many more urgent matters at the moment? The dividing line between the "sheep" and the "goats" in such a context is not belief in Christ or fidelity to the gospel, but the "right" view on political causes and culture wars. In that sense, theism—and indeed Christianity itself—is indeed not even worthy of taking seriously enough to oppose. So I guess the atheist's strategy works. Remember that the apostle Paul not only warned us about being tossed about by winds of doctrine, but that this can come through "human cunning, by craftiness in deceitful schemes" (Eph. 4:14).

This can happen to you in ways that are, at first, imperceptible to you. The gospel of Mark records that after Jesus fed four thousand people, with seven baskets full of broken pieces left over, Jesus' disciples worried and were discussing how they had only one loaf of bread with them in their boat. Jesus said to them, "Beware of the leaven of the Pharisees and the leaven of Herod" (Mark 8:15). What Jesus was warning against was not that the disciples would ideologically align with those two worldviews. In fact, that would have been almost impossible since they were diametrically opposed. The Pharisees were devoted to the kingship of the House of David, as promised in the Law and Prophets, and so chafing under the occupation of the Gentile Romans. Herod, on the other hand, was a puppet of Rome, a client whose ambition was served by his acquiescence to and cooperation with Rome. Jesus called the disciples to be wary but not scared of what was scaring them (running out of bread). He said "beware" to the reality that the disciples might not be defeated by Herod or the Pharisees, but that they would become *like* them. To show this, he used the imagery of "leaven" (yeast). This is the very same metaphor he would use elsewhere to describe the kingdom of God (Matt. 13:33; Luke 13:21), because both uses emphasize the way something can work invisibly, under the surface, unnoticed until it changes everything. There's no sign that the disciples had changed their *political* views (and those were contradictory too, both former zealots and former tax collectors). But, like the Pharisees, they were not seeing the signs—blinded by literalism (how could they not see, he asked, that he was not talking about physical bread). And, like Herod, they were following the way of appetite and control. But, meanwhile, they couldn't see all those broken pieces left over: "Having eyes do you not see, and having ears do you not hear? And do you not remember?" (Mark 8:18). Keep reminding yourself of the signposts you have seen, of the witness you've heard, of what matters, of Who matters, above all else.

Recognize True and False Frames of Spiritual Warfare. "Spiritual warfare" is a new enough term—pioneered through the "power evangelism" ideas of the Fuller Theological Seminary school of mission in the 1970s and 1980s—it is almost evangelical slang. Someone might say when a boss upbraids them at work, "I'm really going through spiritual warfare," or when they are feeling tempted to spend their paycheck on lottery tickets and strip-club lap dances, they might say, "Pray for me; this is spiritual warfare." But, even so, the concept behind spiritual warfare is as old as the church itself—older, in fact. Spiritual warfare is biblically revealed to be against "the cosmic powers over this present darkness, against the spiritual forces of evil in the heavenly places" (Eph. 6:12).

Watch, though, when culture wars are defined as spiritual warfare, with human beings as the "demons" to be opposed. That's precisely what can happen when tribalism connects with resentment and resentment connects with fear. Usually, of course, people don't literally mean that their political or cultural opponents are supernatural evil spirits. But metaphors matter. Think of what happens, throughout history, when the metaphors of "rats" or "insects" or "animals" are applied to human beings. Demons, after all, are not just evil. Demons are craftier than human beings, more powerful than human solutions, and, most critically in this discussion, irredeemable. The cross of Christ saves fallen human beings, not fallen angels (Heb. 2:16). We are not called to persuade demons to do the right thing. We are not called to love demons and to bear with them patiently. No one gives an altar call and asks Satan to appear to the tune of "Just as I Am." Demons are to be opposed—full stop. When we confuse this spiritual struggle with our already-existing tribal rivalries, awful things can happen—if only just our ongoing rage and inability to love and pray for and even evangelize those with whom we disagree.

Moreover, we start, then, to lose sight of what spiritual warfare actually is. The biblical language is used to seek to draw on certain aspects of the spiritual in order to apply them to the mundane—in order to make the mundane seem even more spiritually significant. With a Manichean framing, one can tap into the reality of the schemes of the Evil One to defend a very secular idea of paranoia against those human beings who are seen to be plotting in conspiracy to undo whatever is good. This is akin to the modernist minister of the last century who would preach on Easter of the Resurrection as "a new start to your life this year." That sort of tactic doesn't elevate the hearer's new-start resolutions to the status of the bodily Resurrection of Jesus; all it does is reduce Jesus' resurrection, in the minds of those listening, to the hearers' to-do list for the year.

In Jesus' first-century world, the Zealots could assume that spiritual warfare was opposing Rome. The tax collectors could assume that spiritual warfare was opposing anti-Roman insurrectionists. The Sadducees didn't believe in spirits, but if they had, they could assume that spiritual warfare was opposing the Pharisees. And the Pharisees, of course, could assume that spiritual warfare was opposing Jesus (John 7:20). Later in history, people could act as though spiritual warfare was persecuting Jews—picturing Jewish people as less than and simultaneously as more than human. In the bad cases, this leads to bloodshed; in the worst cases, this can lead to genocide. And, in every case, it empties the biblical truth of spiritual warfare of all meaning. The entire point of spiritual warfare is that it is not present or absent based upon tribes or factions. Spiritual warfare is a reality for every person—and shows up both in doing the wrong things the right way but also in doing the right things the wrong way. If spiritual warfare were simply another way of saying "Arguing with each other" or "Owning the libs" or "Raging against the corporate machine" or whatever, spiritual warfare would mean that some people are exempt and other people are unsalvageable, irredeemable. That would mean denying two key elements of the gospel itself—that "all have sinned and fall short of the glory of God" and that "everyone who calls on the name of the Lord will be saved" (Rom. 3:23; 10:13)—at the same time. If you see yourself listening to or speaking of spiritual warfare in this secularized way—pivot. Pivot away from a focus on culture war to a focus on your neighbors as a mission field. Pivot away from seeing human beings as your enemy, and look for the old serpent of Eden.

Believe and Share the Gospel. For many in the post-Christian West, the evangelical Christian emphasis on "sharing the gospel" or "bearing witness to Christ" is itself an indication of the problem. Images come to mind of screaming sidewalk prophets wearing sandwich boards proclaiming "Repent! The End Is Near!" or hellfire-and-brimstone evangelists screaming that their listeners are on the verge of damnation. It is thought Christians who feel the need to persuade others of the truth of their faith are arrogant, believing the way they've found to be the truth for everybody. Moreover, the idea of some people as "saved" and others as "lost" is dehumanizing, one might argue, leading to the bullying of those who do not share one's beliefs. To be sure, there are plenty of examples such critics could marshal—of imperialistic and colonialist Western missions' efforts and, even further back, of forced conversions and inquisitions. It can't be ignored that even Billy Graham—who could hardly be depicted as Torquemada with his Iron Maidens or even as Jonathan Edwards with his rhetoric of spiders held over the flames of hell—called his evangelistic campaigns "crusades."

And yet, personal evangelism is, at its best, an ongoing reminder to evangelical Christians that their neighbors represent a mission field, not a battlefield, and that the gospel goes forward by persuasion, not by intimidation. The sociologist Christian Smith noted that belief in hell leads to increased civility among evangelical Americans. That's because, he argues, few ordinary evangelicals think of hell in the caricature of devils poking people with pitchforks but as eternal separation from God.* Think of the sorts of rhetoric employed by evangelicals in training programs and tracts—"God loves you and has a wonderful plan for your life" or "If God were to ask you why he should admit you to heaven, what would you say?" or "This was my life before I met Christ, here's how I met Christ, this is my life ever since I met Christ" and so on. In whatever articulation, a church trained to bear witness to the gospel can be a church called to rethink the meaning and limits of power. In short, a self-conscious attention to gospel witness can keep posing the real question beneath our ongoing crises: "What if I were to die tonight?"

Peter Berger argued that such a question is, sociologically speaking, at the root of every human religious impulse. He wrote, "Every human society is, in the last resort, men banded together in the face of death. The power of religion depends, in the last resort, upon the credibility of the banners it puts in the hands of men as they stand before death, or more accurately, as they walk, inevitably, toward it."† In the face of death, Berger contended, human beings need to make some sense of their lives, find some meaning in their sufferings. This attempt to overcome the fear of death is not just at the heart of religion, he continued, but at virtually every

<hr>

*Christian Smith, *Christian America? What Evangelicals Really Want* (Berkley: University of California Press, 2000), 81–82.

†Peter Berger, *The Sacred Canopy: Elements of a Sociological Theory of Religion* (New York: Anchor, 1967, 1990), 51.

human attempt at belonging to some collectivity—whether of a national mythology, a tribal connectivity, a defining ideology. While I might die, the subconscious reasoning goes, the "group" is stable and reaches beyond my death into the future. In that sense, there can be a feeling of almost a kind of "everlasting life." In an evangelical Christian rendering, such a notion is literally an eternal life—not for the group, as a group, but for individuals themselves. By conserving the gospel, you remind yourself that you are, yes, a member of various groups and nations, but you are, before all that, crucified with Christ, and raised with him to newness of life.

When rightly defined and balanced with a fuller Christian picture of discipleship, bearing witness to the saving power of the gospel, the possibility of conversion from deadness to newness serves as a sign of the dove that Noah sent from the ark, a bird that returned with an olive leaf—a sign of life on the other side of the wreckage (Gen. 8:11). Culture wars, on the other hand, turn the scouting mission of the church into that of Noah's ravens—those who never returned to the ark because there were plenty of corpses in the water on which to feed. Scavenging off death feels more certain than the seeking of a new creation, but the Holy Spirit that landed on our Lord Jesus at his baptism, the Holy Spirit he sent to enliven and empower us, is a dove, not a raven.

Cultivate Loyalty in Community. For all their talk of "rootedness" and locality, both the leadership and the grassroots of the various blood-and-soil movements are surprisingly rootless. Christian nationalism, blood-and-soil identity politics, and every other self-defining cultural or political category is really rooted in something God created and declared to be good—the longing for membership. And, like every other created reality, this longing can be twisted into something devilish and self-destructive. The reason white nationalists streamed into Charlottesville at the "Unite the Right" rally was over Confederate monuments—and the motivation for those with Tiki torches was not about broadening a vision of community but in restricting it. "You will not replace us; Jews will not replace us," they chanted. The key is the definition of the word *us*.

What the world needs most from evangelical Christians is that we stand by our own gospel. If Freiman is right that the loss of "cross-cutters" is part of the tribalism of the ambient culture, then that's precisely what the gospel—when defined by blood atonement and new birth, rather than by biology, nationality, or political zeal—claims to do. To be "born again" is to be born into *something*, and that something Jesus defined as "the kingdom of God" (John 3:3, 5). And the New Testament defined the kingdom of God as a reality both present and not yet here. The gospel creates a new sense of belonging—into a household of God—but that belonging often requires a breaking with the ways we previously sought to find our identities. Thus, the apostle Peter wrote to first-century Christians that "you were ransomed from the futile ways inherited from your forefathers, not with perishable things such as silver or gold, but with the precious blood of Christ" (1 Pet. 1: 18–19).

Breaking away from futile ways can be hard in a time when so many churches are in a crisis of their own credibility. Community is nonetheless necessary; the church is nonetheless necessary. In discussing how to avoid the pull to what C. S. Lewis called "the Inner Ring" (inclusion in whatever group or tribe from which one fears exclusion), Alan Jacobs reflects on the way that Lewis contrasts "membership" with both solitary isolation and anonymous collectivism.* The church, Scriptures say, is "one body" and each of us "individually members of it" (1 Cor. 12:27). Membership, Lewis says, differs from tribalism or inclusion in a collective because people are not interchangeable units.† The church is a community, but a *personal* community, a temple of the whole, but a temple built with individual *living stones* (1 Pet. 2:5). All this is emphasized in the Bible in the context of spiritual gifts, individually given, intentionally differing, but all for the upbuilding of the community. Membership implies the usefulness and indispensability of every person in the community. If you are to withstand the upheavals of the days to come, seek after that sort of membership, and that means seeking after a church that *needs* you, and in which you need them, a church that doesn't expect you to be a clone of anyone else or a statistic on a spreadsheet.

On a Saturday morning a while back, I roused two of my teenage sons out of bed to attend a prayer breakfast for men at our church. The subject that day would be the question of sexual morality,

---

*Alan Jacobs, *How to Think: A Survival Guide for a World at Odds* (New York: Penguin Random House, 2017), 60.

†Ibid., 61.

especially as related to technology. I thought they needed such equipping and so I took them along. I expected some grumbling about being awakened so early, about missing a Saturday morning, but both of them spoke of the day as spiritually meaningful and invigorating, in ways I never anticipated, that had nothing to do with the subject or with the "content." When the larger group broke up into smaller groups praying at tables, I found myself tearing up seeing men—from seventy on down—dropping all pretense and confessing their various places of need or failure to one another. As the men went one by one around the table, I was already expecting to jump in right before the turn fell to one of my sons, thinking that since they were the only "kids" in the room I would pray on their behalf. I didn't get the chance. Before I knew it, one of my sons was praying for someone else—an older man. I was a little ashamed that I had almost kept this from happening. The older men did not act as though anything at all was unusual about being prayed for by a fourteen-year-old and a sixteen-year-old. They weren't treated as "teenagers" but as fellow sinners and fellow saints, as men with responsibility for everyone else.

Here there was no adult or adolescent, but Christ was all and in all. It occurred to me that this is precisely what God used to make me into a son of the church—the reality not just of being served but of serving, of being taken seriously as someone who was responsible to repent of sin, to encourage the body, to stack chairs for the assembly time, to serve food to the homeless, and on and on. Even the way my home church did "youth night," where I preached as a twelve-year-old and my friends took up the offering and chose the hymns, was not at all the feel of an "Aren't they cute, pretending to be grown-ups!" affair. My church expected that if God was calling me to ministry, that I would have something to say from the Bible, and they would teach me how to do it. They saw me not just as the twelve-year-old I was, but also as the fifty-year-old I now am. That moment of realization, and gratitude, was so embedded in my mind that I honestly believe I will think about it on my deathbed. A renewal of the church into a multigenerational household does not start with better programs or sophisticated strategies, but with our recovering this sense of taking each member of the body seriously, helping to find the ways that God has gifted each person, and then allowing people to need one another again. You might say, "There are no churches like that around me." Then work to make yours like that, or pray for God to put you together with others who see something missing in order to plant one.

In the letters of J. R. R. Tolkien, we find the Inkling writing to a son for whom "the Church which once felt like a refuge, now often feels like a trap." Tolkien told his son to ask first whether the Gospels are fraudulent, if Jesus himself was a fraud. If not, Tolkien wrote, then "exercise the virtue of loyalty, which indeed only becomes a virtue when one is under pressure to desert it."* To do that,

---

*J. R. R. Tolkien, Letter to Michael Tolkien, circa 1967, in *The Letters of J. R. R. Tolkien*, ed. Humphrey Carpenter (Boston: Houghton Mifflin Harcourt, 1981, 2000), 393.

Tolkien recommended that his son find an ordinary parish, filled with people who don't meet his ideals, but filled with people unkempt and unimpressive. I would argue that where one is most likely to find a community that transcends the tribal and political idolatry of the moment is serving among those who are genuinely hurting. Serve in a rescue mission or a home for abused women or among recovering alcoholics. Find a people not just with whom to identify yourself, but to lose yourself in by serving them. And find a people who really know what it means when they sing, "I once was lost but now I'm found." You'll be more likely there to be reminded that the same is true of you.

Rekindle Awe. Every once in a while, you might hear someone suggest that some of our hymns are unhealthy and self-loathing—"that saved a wretch like me," "for such a worm as I." And yet, none of those songs speaks of one's own depravity in these ways in order to create shame and guilt; just the opposite. These songs are written, and meant to be sung, in the context of *awe.* "I stand amazed in the presence of Jesus the Nazarene . . ." The gospel announces that we are sinners in need of redemption, but also assumes that (if only at the most subconscious level of the human psyche) we already know that. The recitation of the gospel—including our own inability to help ourselves—must always, if faithful to the Christian tradition, result in the same sort of awe as the prophet Isaiah expressed when he saw the glory of God filling the temple, "Woe is me! For I am lost; for I am a man of unclean lips and I dwell in the midst of a people of unclean lips" (Isa. 6:5). Framed by the Christian gospel, this understanding calls the community to walk away from the tyranny of the ego and to stand before the vastness of the mercy of God in Christ. Now, as one who believes the gospel, I believe that everyone needs this. But even those who disagree with me on that should see that they need evangelical Christians like me to believe it.

What the Christian church learned in the first century was that fragmentation was a question of "sorting" before it was a question of "splitting." In saying "I follow Paul" and "I follow Cephas," one was swearing a loyalty and merging one's own conscience into a herd defined by something short of Christ (1 Cor. 1:10–17). Biologists and psychologists would find that unsurprising. Many of them would say that human beings evolved with a need to differentiate between the "in group" and the "out group," the familiar and the strange. It's "natural," some would tell us, to ask the question of the young lawyer to Jesus: "Who is my neighbor?" All of us would agree that this sort of "hive mind" is a necessary function at times. If a fire breaks out in your Sunday morning service, you don't want a robust discussion about possible means of escape. You want the whole gathering, as one, to suspend their personal judgments and move. The problem that we see right now—ratcheted up to an unprecedented level by social media—is that there seems to be no off switch for the hive mind. Social psychologist Jonathan Haidt points to research showing that one factor is most important in "resetting" people, to shift them from a hive mind of tribalism, and that factor is awe. Haidt defines awe as an emotion triggered by two experiences: vastness ("something overwhelms us and makes us feel small") and accommodation (so outside of our normal mental structures that we must change them in order to make room for it).*

Haidt, of course, is an atheist and so he proposes all sorts of ways to pursue awe, to find the self by eclipsing the self: psychedelic drugs, etc. And yet, here again is an aspect of evangelical Christianity that often has made us stumble but just might get at something we need. Much critique has gone into the "emotional" nature of much of evangelical worship, and rightly so. We can so seek an "experience" in worship that we neglect the truth that God is most often present in the ordinary, not in ecstasy. That search for an experience can leave less emotionally expressive people wondering, wrongly, if they really can worship at all. It can become a driver of mass marketing for those who know how to manipulate moods with worship songs. All these critiques are true, and many more. And yet.

The Jewish philosopher Leon Kass draws on the biblical scene of Moses at the Burning Bush in order to contrast "Egyptian wonder"—at, for instance, controlling the life-giving, life-destroying power of fire through a sun-god—with "Hebraic awe." The awe comes for Moses, he argues, not just in the curiosity of the sight—a bush on fire and not consumed—but that a voice from this bush addresses Moses personally, by name, "not once but twice, emphatically and with authority." This sort of awe, Kass argues, is quite different from

---

*Jonathan Haidt, *The Righteous Mind: Why Good People Are Divided by Politics and Religion* (New York: Pantheon, 2012), 244.

curiosity, because it elicits both a drawing ("Moses . . .") and a distance ("Take off your shoes and come no nearer"). This does not, he contends, "like simple fear or terror, lead us to flee." Instead: "We are both attracted and repelled; we want both to approach and to stand back; we want to oscillate in place, bound in relation to the thing that defies our comprehension and makes us feel small. We hide our face, but we hold our ground. Paradoxically, thanks to awe-fear-reverence and the bond it builds across the unbridgeable divide, we also feel less small."[*]

This is a God who, for those of us who follow Jesus, is beyond our highest thoughts and yet near to us—a God whose glory we have seen in the face of Jesus Christ—a God who is holy, holy, holy, and yet calls us, by name, "Come, follow me." The sort of awe with which we see God is infinitely greater than any we have in the presence of another human being. But each human being, the Bible tells us, is a signpost of that very God—and we approach each person, then, with a sense of familiarity but never with a sense of mastery. This is perhaps why so many people come to faith after they have children—not, as I previously thought, because they think they should "raise them in church," but because they see in this person in front of them more than just a bundle of neurons, a carrier of DNA, but something mysterious and wondrous. Sometimes, in those moments, one feels not just love but awe—and a longing to

---

[*]Leon Kass, *Founding God's Nation: Reading Exodus* (New Haven: Yale University Press, 2021), 63–64.

---

find someone to thank. Like anything else, the gospel itself can become so assumed and familiar that we lose the sheer amazement in the face of it all. Maybe the reason we as Christians seem to seethe with resentment and find our loyalties in tribal factions and ideologies is because we've lost that sense of standing in worshipful awe before a God who is not a set of doctrines or a motivation for institutional survival or a national deity or a political mascot. Maybe our clamoring for those sorts of hive minds is because we've become bored—unsurprised by joy, unamazed by grace. Perhaps the answer for awful times is an awe-full solution.

Make Peace with Homelessness. By this I don't mean the unhoused around you, but the metaphorical sense of "homelessness" many now feel—with their political parties, with their religious traditions, maybe even with their own extended families or churches. The upheavals of the past few years have done just that. A couple of years ago, I was speaking at a warmhearted, gospel-fueled Anglican gathering. Afterward, I was greeted by what seemed to be hundreds of people, each one of whom came to Christ and grew up in a Southern Baptist church. The startling thing to me is that not one of these people was bitter, and no one wanted to commiserate about what a nuclear-reactor-level meltdown the Southern Baptist Convention had become. Instead, they wanted to reminisce—about those cookies and punch at Vacation Bible School, about the Sword Drills, about "Training Union" and "RAs" and "Acteens" and "Centrifuge" and a host of other words that one would only know in the linguistic subculture that was the Southern Baptist world of a certain moment in time. Each one of them loved the Anglican church they now attended, or led. They found rich resources in Anglicanism that they didn't have in Baptist life. They wouldn't go back. But, still, they didn't feel completely at home. As one woman said, with a twinkle in her eyes, "I keep my Book of Common Prayer on my desk in front of me all the time, but there's the *Baptist Hymnal* next to it."

Even people who haven't changed churches have felt this sense of disruption, of new relationships formed, old relationships dissolved, of not quite belonging all the way to the people for whom you now vote or the part of the country in which you live. And for many of you, you would say, "And I never changed. I wasn't the one that moved." That is painful and disorienting, as I know. If, as I was waking out of anesthesia after surgery, the nurse asked, "What religion are you?" I have no doubt that I would say, "Southern Baptist." Maybe, though, this is an opportunity to rethink how we imagine "home" and how we think of "exile."

Before you do, though, choose your metaphors carefully. You may be experiencing "exile" of a sort, but you are not experiencing "occupation." After all, "occupation" implies that a hostile force has invaded one's own territory—holding a people hostage in their own land. This is, at several points, a reality in the biblical story of the people of God. This is the reason why, for instance, the question the religious leaders posed to Jesus about whether to pay taxes to Caesar was so fraught. To say yes to that question, in the mindset of many in first-century Israel, would be to affirm the occupation of Rome over the land that was to be governed, not by a puppet government directed by Caesar, but by the House of David. Jesus looked past this temporal occupation toward a deeper, more primal one—the internal occupation represented by the strong man's house being overtaken (Matt. 12:29). The question of occupation, though, was hardly an unreasonable one, or an unspiritual one. It was a question of God's justice—how could Israel's God let this go on?— and a matter of the humiliation of a people. The matter of how to deal with this occupation could lead to some of the most dangerous rifts among the occupied people—with a spectrum ranging from insurrectionists such as Barabbas to Zealots such as Simon and then all the way over to collaborators such as Matthew and Zacchaeus. In an occupation, the problem is the occupier—displacing them from their illegitimate rule. In occupation, the "outsiders" are the ones who are alien to the land. In exile, though, it's the "insiders" who are learning to navigate a strange place.

Peter addressed the church as "elect exiles of the Dispersion" (1 Pet. 1:1) and told them to "conduct yourselves with fear throughout the time of your exile" (1 Pet. 1:17). This was not a recognition of how *different* the first-century church was but how much the same. They were not to find their pattern of life in the "futile ways inherited from your forefathers" (1 Pet. 1:18). The "exile" of which Peter spoke did not mean that they lacked a belonging, but instead that they had a *different* belonging—to "a chosen race, a royal priesthood, a holy nation" (1 Pet. 2:9). This exile means that, like Daniel in Babylon, the objective is not to remove Nebuchadnezzar from his throne or to govern the Babylonian Empire. The objective is quite contrary to that: it is for the exiles to avoid becoming *like* the Babylonians. Peter's urging of the church to be "sojourners and exiles," then, was about seeing that their real problem was not the emperor or the culture around them. They could show honor to everyone, including the emperor. Their problem instead was to "abstain from the passions of the flesh, which wage war against your soul" (1 Pet. 2:11). If they were under occupation—in the sense of a Land of Promise dominated by enemies—then they would either seek to absorb into the larger culture or to rage against the occupiers. Neither was the case. They were both to keep their conduct "among the Gentiles honorable" (1 Pet. 2:12) and to see to it that their obedience was to God not to that audience.

Again, can "exile" language be used dangerously—to convey a sense of resentment at a loss of cultural power? Of course it can, in the same way that "holiness" can be used dangerously to suggest self-righteousness or perfection or the way that "mission" can be used to suggest colonization. Those dangerous uses, though, require that one doesn't know what those words mean in a biblical context. In the exile, the people of Israel were reminded constantly that their plight was not the result of the Babylonians and couldn't be resolved by finding some other power (Egypt, say, or Assyria) to combat the Babylonians. *God* was responsible for their exile. That's why the calling of God's people, then, was not to find their own Nebuchadnezzar. Their responsibility was to *repent*, and to reclaim their own distinctiveness as the people of God. Moreover, the language of exile clarifies that the issue is not just one of getting back home. Both Jeremiah and Ezekiel made clear to the exiles that they couldn't go back home; God's glory had left the temple—not because he had been chased away by the external forces but because he had left due to the sins of his own people (Ezek. 10; Jer. 7). That's the bad news. But the good news is that if God was the one who sent his people out into exile, then he was with them there. They could find him there, and sing the Lord's song in a strange land. They could plant houses and have babies and adapt to some of the externalities of Babylonian life (Daniel could be called a Babylonian name, for instance, and serve in Nebuchadnezzar's court) while refusing to yield to the expected idolatries or to the more subtle pull to lose the "strangeness" and "distinctiveness" of their Abrahamic identity.

The point of "exile" language is exactly the opposite of the idea that Western Christians should lament or resent losing a "Christian culture." The point is that in every place and every culture, from the first to the second comings of Jesus, *every* Christian community are to be "strangers and exiles." If we can look backward and find some time when we were not so, it's because we are accommodated to idolatry—just of a previous Nebuchadnezzar rather than the one in front of us in the moment. And if we can look forward to a time when we can displace the sense of marginalization and find a cultural "home" in the span of history as we know it, then that too is because we are accommodated to idolatry—just that of a future Nebuchadnezzar. If exile language is used to bemoan a "darkening" or "growingly hostile" culture, rather than to see our situation as fundamentally the same as every other era before us, then we don't understand what the Bible means by exile. Exile language does away with both a sense of entitlement and with a siege mentality. We don't look to merge into whatever seems "normal" around us—and we don't rage when we're not accommodated there. We see our normal situation as not occupation but pilgrimage.

"These all died in faith, not having received the things promised, but having seen them and greeted them from afar, and having acknowledged that they were strangers and exiles on the earth," the writer of Hebrews told us. "For people who speak thus make it clear that they are seeking a homeland. If they had been thinking of that land from which they had gone out, they would have had opportunity to return. But as it is, they desire a better country, that is, a heavenly one" (Heb. 11:13–16). An exilic identity does not mean "Oh no! We're marginalized! How can we fix it?" An exilic identity asks, "Why do I not seem more marginalized than I do? Is it because I've adapted my own appetites to the degree that I can no longer feel the longing that drives me onward into the unknown?" The danger for us at the moment is not that Christians will see themselves as exiled in a far country, but that they will see the United States or Canada or wherever they are as the Promised Land. Such means either that they embrace everything around them as milk and honey from God or that they seek to uproot the Amalekites and Philistines that have taken "our country" away from us. That's a sign that we are not exiled enough.

The evangelical missionary martyr Jim Elliot wrote in his diary that the blessing of Abraham started when the patriarch "owned his strangerhood."* Elliot resolved that so must he. The idea that we are pilgrims and wayfarers is really about *conversion*. We are born into the kingdom of God, and so we are experiencing both some of the realities of the kingdom now *and* the longing for those which are yet to come. That reality makes up the paradox of what it means to be born again in the first place. We are in the world, and yet not of it. We are sinners, yet justified. We are dying, yet resurrected. Whatever the truth of the sociological claim about the need for "cross-cutters," that we discussed before, we can certainly affirm a different sort of "cross-cutting"—and that is those whose identities are formed first by an actual cross, by Christ and him crucified (Gal. 2:20). If this is the case—and our lives are in the context of eternity—we need not worry about whether we are politically "homeless." Only those with no home are frantic to find one. That means that no person or ideology or movement, short of Christ himself, can claim the totality of our identities. We can work with people—even with whom we disagree—on matters, issue by issue, but we don't belong to them. We will not be crushed when we see

---

*Jim Elliot, January 17, 1948, in *The Journals of Jim Elliot*, ed. Elisabeth Elliot (Grand Rapids: Baker, 1978), 12.

people who agree with us on some things disagree with us on others. And we won't be terrified when we find that people who disagree with us on most things agree with us on something—for fear that we will be accused of "disloyalty." Once you own your exile, the threat of exile is meaningless. No one can do to you what's already been done. That can give you the freedom, then, to unclench your fists and love—even those who are threatening you with exile.

And we can be freed from the emotional expectations of political identities of various sorts, which are posed in terms of exuberant triumph ("We won!") or apocalyptic despair ("We are about to lose our entire society!"). Both the exuberance and the despair are exhausting and, even worse, either can be used to justify all sorts of things we never thought we would affirm, or things we never imagined we would deny. The way to do that is to remind yourself where home really is, and pray and meditate upon that until you start to long for it. That's the first step to declaring independence from the kind of culture where it's always Election Day, and never Easter.

CHAPTER FOUR

LOSING OUR INTEGRITY

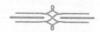

How Morality Can Save Us from Hypocrisy

I t's not unusual for a church to wonder whether a youth minister is going liberal on them, or sometimes maybe even the preacher. But when a church decides Jesus might be going liberal, we are really entering a new era. In his novel *Jayber Crow*, Wendell Berry writes of Jayber, a barber in Kentucky, cutting the hair of Troy, a man who was convinced that they were surrounded by Communists and that they should be rounded up and shot. Jayber stopped, looked at Troy and said, "Love your enemies, bless them that curse you, do good to them that hate you." Troy replied, "Where did you get that crap?" When Jayber said, "Jesus Christ," Troy could only respond, "Oh." Jayber reflects: "It would have been a great moment in the history of Christianity, except that I did not love Troy."* When I first read this, over twenty years ago, I did what

---

*Wendell Berry, *Jayber Crow* (Washington, DC: Counterpoint, 2000), 287.

I'd never done before with a piece of Wendell Berry writing—I rolled my eyes. Berry was not wrong, I thought, that Jesus' Sermon on the Mount is a challenge to any culture, including the Bible Belt culture he was depicting. Still, I thought, the moment was a little too on the nose to be realistic. I don't think that now.

Pastor after pastor has described for me almost identical experiences in which they would parenthetically quote, somewhere in a sermon, a statement along the lines of "turn the other cheek," only to be met after the service with irate church members demanding to know where they had gotten the "liberal talking points." At first, I chalked up such controversies to biblical illiteracy, assuming that once a "Bible-believing Christian" discovered that the objectionable words were direct biblical quotations from Jesus Christ that he or she would respond sheepishly, like Troy: "Oh." Instead, though, often the angry Christians knew exactly who had said those words. As one congregant said to his pastor, "We've tried the 'turn the other cheek' stuff. It doesn't work; it's time now to fight." We have arrived at the point at which, for many people who name the name of Jesus Christ, Christlikeness is compromise. How did this happen?

Around the world right now, if one asks what comes to mind when a person hears the words *American evangelical*, the answer probably will not be "justification through faith alone," or "the people who do prison ministry and disaster relief." The answer probably won't even be "a commitment to traditional family values and the sanctity of human life." The answer will very likely be "Donald

Trump." When I hear of a college campus ministry taking the word *evangelical* out of their name, it's virtually never because they think people will be uncomfortable with biblical inerrancy or world missions, or even with the more controversial aspects of traditional Christian sexual ethics. It's almost always because new students who arrive on campus assume an "evangelical" ministry will be handing out red "Make America Great Again" baseball caps with the paperback Bibles and the praise chorus sheets. The reason this identification sticks with so many people is not because of the overwhelming majority of white evangelicals who voted for this particular candidate, but the seeming cognitive dissonance of choosing a promiscuous, profane, thrice-married casino magnate to restore morality to America. While some people outside the church might just shrug their shoulders at the perplexity of that, others will say that it proves what they've suspected all along—that evangelical Christians are hypocrites and interested not in morality but in political power and cultural dominance. That's not an unreasonable assumption. After all, for decades, they heard evangelical Christians say that "character matters."

During the Bill Clinton era, for instance, conservative Christians made the case, loudly, that private character matters for public leadership. Richard John Neuhaus, the founder of *First Things*, acknowledged that shady characters had always been and would always be in American life. "The difference is that our intellectual leadership, the media, and the then-mainline churches did not tell the morally slovenly sector of the electorate that they were right in their indifference to character," Neuhaus wrote.* Jerry Falwell Sr. called for the resignations of both President Clinton and New York City mayor Rudy Giuliani, since their marital infidelities, in Falwell's opinion, disqualified them from office and "lowered the bar for political officeholders in America."† Carl F. H. Henry, the first editor in chief of *Christianity Today* and perhaps the most prominent American evangelical theologian of the twentieth century, said that "public virtue depends on private character," and that if Christians ever started to excuse malformed character because the social and political stakes are high, "the wrong priority prevails. Supposedly in the name of civilizational rescue, we repeat the same confused priorities that have precipitated and contributed to the existing cultural decline."‡ Historian Kristin Kobes Du Mez concludes, "Among Clinton's evangelical critics, it appears that their concern with Clinton's predatory behavior was more about Clinton than about predatory behavior."§

By 2016, this was clear, even to some of us who hadn't wanted to believe it before. Perhaps this was most clearly seen in October

---

*Richard John Neuhaus, "A Mirror of the National Soul," *First Things*, March 1997.

†Quoted in Joe Scarborough, "Trump Has Made Courage Scarce," *Seattle Times*, December 23, 2019.

‡Carl F. H. Henry, *Has Democracy Had Its Day?* (Nashville: Christian Life Commission of the Southern Baptist Convention, 1996), 61.

§Kristin Kobes Du Mez, *Jesus and John Wayne: How White Evangelicals Corrupted a Faith* (New York: Norton, 2020), 144.

of 2016, only weeks before the election, when audio was released of Donald Trump boasting of the fact that he moved on a married woman "like a bitch." This part was no surprise. He had, after all, consistently bragged of his sexual exploits—in his own books and on shock-jock radio shows. What was different here was that Trump was glorifying sexual assault. "I'm automatically attracted to beautiful—I just start kissing them. It's like a magnet. Just kiss. I don't even wait," he said in leaked audio from behind the scenes on the *Access Hollywood* television show. "When you're a star they let you do it. You can do anything. Grab them by the pussy. You can do anything." I realize as I write this that this must be the first time that I have typed some of those words before. That's one more way that Donald Trump has changed my life.

Another way that it changed my life was the fury with which my fellow evangelical Christians responded to my comments that Trump was morally unfit for leadership. That part wasn't surprising since I had been saying the same thing since the billionaire had descended the escalator to announce his candidacy in 2015. When the *Access Hollywood* tape was released, I counseled friends who also were opposed to Trump, to have empathy with their Trump-supporting friends and fellow leaders. They would be shell-shocked and rattled, I said, and some of them will be grieving so no one should say anything that even remotely could be interpreted as "I told you so." I needn't have worried. Within hours, the old-guard Religious Right was out defending Trump, even when his own running mate was refusing to do so publicly and his own political party was running legal scenarios for replacing him on the ballot. As soon as I made critical comments about the atrocity of sexual assault and harassment, a fellow Southern Baptist entity leader was on the phone screaming that I had betrayed "our side," before hanging up on me. More disorienting was when an elderly lady who had taught me the Bible in Sunday school as a child sent me a message denouncing me for betraying our people.

What was perhaps most surprising was that none of the leaders defending Trump or attacking those of us who couldn't support him made the case that the audio was fake or inaccurate, or even that Trump had repented and changed. What they said was "grow up." The audio was "locker room talk," and the stakes were too high to worry about such things. All the tropes used so far to excuse the nativism, the cruelty, the crazed public and private temperament were trotted out: Trump's not a Sunday school teacher or a new King David or pagan deliverer Cyrus who would free God's people from exile. After the *Access Hollywood* tapes were released, one Religious Right leader told Christian students that they must use their "moral imagination" to see that they had no choice but to support Trump. "Refusing to muddy our boots with the mud and mire of politics is simply not an option for a follower of Christ," he said, as though the hesitancy to support Trump came from an Amish-type disengagement with the civic order.* "It's a lot easier to opt out and

---

*Jeremy W. Peters, *Insurgency: How Republicans Lost Their Party and Got Everything They Ever Wanted* (New York: Crown, 2022), 255.

take the Pontius Pilate, position and say, 'I'm going to wash my hands of this,'" another prominent evangelical said after *Access Hollywood*. Pontius Pilate, remember, washed his hands of responsibility *for the crucifixion of Jesus Christ.*

One reason given for white evangelical support for Trump was that these Christians were voting for the "lesser of two evils." And many were. For some, it was the fact that Trump's Supreme Court nominees would be far more likely than Hillary Clinton's to reverse *Roe v. Wade* (which of course they later did) and to protect the religious liberty of faith-based institutions to operate according to their beliefs. I could see the reason behind such a calculation, even though I didn't share it. What concerned me was that, first of all, this moral calculation is precisely the sort of moral relativism and situational ethics these very same people warned us would come from the secularists and leftists. There are, of course, no perfect candidates (or pastors or spouses or human beings), but surely there is some line in which a person's character is too flawed to be fit to lead, whatever the consequences might be. Military service is another office of public responsibility. One need not approve of everything a general decides in order to be a faithful soldier for one's country. But if one's army commands a Christian to make the decision either to slaughter innocent noncombatants or desert and sign up with the enemies of one's country, a Christian can't merely choose the least bad of these options. He would have to conclude that both options are wrong and his conscience could not be implicated in either. He would have to conscientiously object. Along with the slander of lying for God's glory, Paul quoted those who would say, "Why not do evil that good may come?" (Rom. 3:8). Later he tells us that vengeance cannot bring about good because of the command: "Do not be overcome by evil, but overcome evil with good" (Rom. 12:21).

What worried me also was that I knew that the "lesser of two evils" argument rarely stays that way. Hannah Arendt famously warned that "those who choose the lesser evil quickly forget that they chose evil."* That proved to be true, and increasingly true. What many in the grassroots movement didn't know was that a lot of the most enthusiastic Trump supporters among evangelicals did not dispute at all my contention that his character is perverted or that his personality is disordered. After a meeting at which one mega-church pastor upbraided me for not supporting Trump, the pastor sighed and said, "He's an evil, immoral man." During the Trump administration, this leader did not, in fact, praise policies he supported while denouncing others that were at odds with what he defined as biblical morality, even on matters he had long publicly supported—whether that was Trump's refusal to denounce white supremacists after the Charlottesville rally or the separation of migrant children from their mothers at the southern border or the payment of money to a porn star with whom Trump allegedly had an affair. Instead, this leader praised Trump consistently on

*Hannah Arendt, "Personal Responsibility Under Dictatorship," in *Responsibility and Judgment*, ed. Jerome Kohn (New York: Schocken, 2003), 36.

television as a great president and as a champion for the values we cherish. Some Christian leaders pronounced him, a self-described unrepentant man, a "baby Christian." This was not a quibble about what is the lesser of two evils and whether we should gamble with such for the sake of the Supreme Court. This is a question of the very definition—overheard by the world of our mission field—of what is the gospel itself, and what does it mean to be saved or lost. In the twentieth century, a fundamentalist leader defined a "compromising evangelical" as "a fundamentalist who says to a liberal, 'I'll call you a Christian if you'll call me a scholar.'" It seems now that we have some evangelicals who are willing to say to politicians, "I'll call you a Christian if you'll just call me." We were now, at long last, all contestants on *The Apprentice*, clamoring to make the cut to the next episode and fearful of hearing the words *you're fired*.

The "lesser of two evils" argument was not the primary reason behind at least white evangelical leaders' support for Trump, and wherever it was in the grassroots, the mindset would quickly dissipate, and not just with this one candidate. During a tumultuous United States Senate race in 2017, an Alabama Baptist deacon told a journalist that credible charges that an "evangelical" candidate had sexually pursued minor-age girls would not be a disqualifier for his vote. "I believe in innocent until proven guilty, but even if he's guilty, I'll back him all the way," the deacon said. "I still feel he's a Christian man—and nobody's perfect."* This was hardly an outlier.

---

*Peters, *Insurgency*, 28

Public polling demonstrated that evangelical Christians shifted their viewpoints dramatically on whether personal character is relevant to public leadership. In order to stop the Clintons, we had to learn how to ask what the meaning of the word *is* is. In order to stop moral relativism, we had to give up on objective morality.

Clinton—whether Bill or Hillary—was not the best callback from the 1990s to show us what was happening with evangelicals on moral character. For that we would need to turn to former professional football player O. J. Simpson, whose trial for murdering his ex-wife and another man dominated the cable news networks early in the Clinton era. Writer Chuck Klosterman argues that the most important facet of how this case divided America was the fact that Simpson could not have been more obviously guilty "outside of O. J. wearing a body camera while performing the decapitation." He writes that the "obviousness of Simpson's guilt was key to the postmodern drama" of it all because it created "a game show quality to watching the trial: Could Simpson's 'dream team' of defense lawyers win an argument that seemed impossible to take seriously?" In the end, Klosterman contends, the argument turned out to be a "math equation" of weighing Simpson's guilt against the history of racism in America.* The fact that most people knew that he probably did slaughter two human beings was beside the point. Is there any real doubt that had Simpson been a white police officer and had

---

*Chuck Klosterman, *The Nineties: A Book* (New York: Penguin Random House, 2022), 260.

murdered two Black people, many of those arguing for "justice" and "law and order" would have reversed positions to defend him? The morality is dependent on the outcomes, and the good or evil of the outcomes themselves is determined by tribal allegiance.

So how does this happen? Throughout the Trump era, one consistent refrain from white evangelicals was, "We're electing a president, not a pastor." And yet, the terrifying reality is that a significant portion of white evangelicals were treating Trump *exactly* as they would a pastor. Several years ago, I was talking with an older man in my Southern Baptist tradition about a pastor who had been caught in what we euphemistically call "a moral failure." I said something about his wrecking his life and ministry when the older man corrected me: "Oh, he'll be back in ministry." When I said that many Baptist churches would be reluctant to call a minister with so public a scandal, he assured me that many would. "Besides," he said, "the pattern is always the same after adultery with our people. White-collar pastors become Episcopalians and blue-collar pastors become Pentecostals." Now, this is manifestly unfair to both the Anglican Communion and to the very large community of faithful churches in the Pentecostal/charismatic wings of the church. Still, he was referring to the extremes, the often caricatured versions of both traditions, in which one could escape accountability in what seem to be very different ways.

What this man called "Episcopalian" was less about that specific denomination than about the leftward march on sexual ethics generally in many mainline churches. A fallen pastor might find a church who would blame his affair on a "repressive" view of sex within the evangelical and fundamentalist worlds, or the pastor might, in some context, declare himself polyamorous. What this man meant by "Pentecostal" was the world of prosperity-gospel in which the more pastors are called out for abusive behavior or for financial grift or for sexual promiscuity, the more they rail against "the ungodly" who are trying to take down "God's anointed." In some of these contexts, even the most obvious of character flaws can be overlooked as long as one keeps drawing a crowd and keeps a paradoxical blend of utopianism ("have faith and you can be healed and/or rich; buy my prayer cloths") with catastrophism ("the end is near; buy my bunker food supplies!").

What the older man told me had enough anecdotes to be plausible, although there were plenty of people from my tradition who became Episcopalians because they became convinced by the beauty of its liturgy or the theology of the Book of Common Prayer, and plenty of people became Pentecostals because they were convinced that all the spiritual gifts are meant for today or by the freedom of the worship styles, et cetera. In fact, in Africa, Asia, and Latin America, the evangelical growth and church-planting is largely due to Pentecostalism, while the archbishop of Canterbury says that the average Anglican is not a gentleman in east London but a sub-Saharan African woman living on less than four dollars a day. Meanwhile there are a multitude of examples within almost every strain of evangelical Christianity of serious character issues in ministry waved away because of the minister's giftedness and "success." Those empowering such behavior often go from "We don't like these aspects, but we want the pastor to succeed in the good things" to "Well, I don't like his tone, but you have to admit he says what he thinks" to "Take him seriously, not literally" to "He's shaking things up! He's not politically correct" to "When you're a star they'll let you do it." This eclipse of character through power happened in many evangelical circles well before it was applied to politics. And while we conservative evangelicals often (and often rightly) criticized the mainline for accommodating to "the culture," is it any less being "conformed to the world" when one accommodates to a subculture? What about when the accommodation is not (at least publicly) about sex but about wrath, greed, and dishonesty? In either case, does not one end up with what Daniel Patrick Moynihan referred to in another context as "defining deviancy down"?*

To really understand the shift here, it's essential that you see the role played by the rhetoric of catastrophism. As Wendell Berry warned: "The most destructive of ideas is that extraordinary times justify extraordinary measures. This is the ultimate relativism, and we are hearing it from all sides."† After all, the way we came to this point was through a sort of catastrophism. The Republic is "Flight 93," highjacked by terrorists; therefore we must turn it around by

---

*Daniel Patrick Moynihan, "Defining Deviancy Down," *The American Scholar* 62, no. 1 (1993): 17–30.

†Wendell Berry, *A Continuous Harmony: Essays Cultural and Agricultural* (Washington, DC: Shoemaker and Hoard, 1972), 159.

any means necessary. We must make transactional political alliances, even ones that swallow up the identity of our witness, or we won't have a country anymore. We must tread very lightly around the biblical teachings on justice or we will lose "the base," and with them the resources to evangelize the world. We must not ask too many questions about spiritual or sexual abuse, even within our churches, or we will sacrifice this or that urgent ministry; we might lose our church. In almost every character meltdown—whether in a church or a ministry or a denomination—there was a sense that those issues could be dealt with, but not in the middle of this emergency—and it didn't matter whether the "emergency" was a theological battle or a building campaign or a sudden growth cycle or the culture war enemies out to destroy us. Those kinds of emergencies never end or, if they do, are replaced immediately by some other emergency. It was in the church that many learned the principle of "This person is of repulsive character, but he has all the right enemies," so he can be trusted to fight the right people and to leave unaccountable the right people. What's lost in this is that this mentality is exactly what empowers, for instance, an abortion culture. The woman in the waiting room of the abortion clinic, or the man who took her there, don't necessarily think that abortion is right or even morally neutral. Often they believe it is wrong—maybe they even think it is the taking of innocent human life—but, they conclude, the alternatives are worse. When looking at a life of poverty or responsibility for a child they do not feel equipped to parent, they conclude that their life is a "Flight 93" emergency.

Over a decade ago, a historian argued that the Southern Baptist Convention's decades-long skirmish between "conservatives" and "moderates" actually "stood for broader trends in American political life: activists driven to radical, absolutist positions and the casting of one's political opponents not as fellow citizens engaged in spirited debate but as traitors, heretics, and pariahs based on the conviction that compromise is defeat and empathy for fellow human beings a fall from moral righteousness."* At the time I first read this, I discounted it as unaware of the actual theological matters at debate, such as the meaning of biblical authority. I was, and am, a conservative on those theological issues, but I can see how we pioneered many of the same patterns that later showed up, with full force, in the rest of American life. When someone put on a board or on a committee was described as "a warhorse of the conservative resurgence" or "has blood on his hands" (which was always said, mind you, as a compliment), we knew that meant "He (or she, but usually he) is mean and angry" and/or "He's a little bit crazy, but he's one of us." We could see leaders whose character we would never admire, and to whom we would never go for spiritual counsel, but who would make the right appointments or fight the right people. The stakes were so high, we were told and told ourselves, that we didn't always have the luxury of leaders with personal integrity or sanity; that could all come later, once the "battles" were

---

*Robert O. Self, *All in the Family: The Realignment of American Democracy Since the 1960s* (New York: Farrar, Straus & Giroux, 2012), 366.

won. One leader told me how dangerous a particular theologian on the "liberal" side was because she was always there with her students when someone lost a job or suffered a miscarriage. This meant, he implied, that she elicited a type of loyalty that would lead those students away from orthodoxy. I would disagree with the "liberal" on virtually all the "fundamentals" of the faith and would not want her serving on a faculty training ministers, but was this really the choice? Was the "binary" between "unorthodox" people who were loving and kind and "orthodox" who were angry, calculating, and willing to do anything to win? When a member of Congress told me about the books on narcissistic personality disorder he was reading in order to better deal with President Trump, I realized that I had read all those same books in order to deal with some Southern Baptist leaders. I didn't hear the language of ". . . but he fights!" in reference to a badly damaged and demagogic human being in any presidential election, but in the context of my own network of churches.

In our mythology, two men had "saved the convention from liberalism." They were, in the way we told the history, our Luther and Calvin. They were revered by many, though the higher one went in the denomination, the more one could see the respect evaporate, and be replaced only by fear. No one wanted to get flowers delivered from one of them, said to be a sign that one was "dead to him," and, if dead to him, then dead to Baptist life. More than that, one didn't want to get a fiery letter or phone call from one of their wives; ironically enough, these wives would often call to yell at and threaten men for not being sufficiently committed to male head-ship over women. In the "apocalypse" of the post-2016 era, one of these men would be accused in a civil lawsuit of sexually abusing young men and the other revealed in emails to have threatened to "break down" a rape victim for telling her story. Video also showed up in the press of this same leader making what can only be called sexualized comments about the attractiveness of a teenage girl. The foot soldiers devoted to these two men were, at the very same time, engaged in everything from questioning the veracity or sta-bility of sexual abuse survivors to harassing them online. In the meantime, the more "normal" leaders were obsessed with the fact that a woman spoke from the pulpit in one church on Mother's Day. I was angry. "It was all a fraud," I said to a friend. "These peo-ple used biblical inerrancy the way the medieval church used purgatory—to sell a different sort of indulgence, to inquisition a different set of heretics, and to build a different St. Peter's Cathe-dral." But the truth is, I should have known. Every time we would see that these men lacked the basic spirituality we would expect of a deacon, I told myself, "Well, they gave their lives to saving the denomination for biblical orthodoxy so give them that." When they would say something bordering on outright racism, we would tell ourselves, "They're old. They'll be retired soon. Everybody has a grandpa or a great-uncle like this." In all this I was somewhere be-tween "Let's go with the lesser of two evils" and "If you're a star, they'll let you do it."

When referring to the Trump opposition among conservatives

in the political space, one satirist created a logo for the "Leopards Eating People's Faces Party" with the tagline "It's Not Like They're Going to Eat *My* Face!" The joke was effective because it was true enough to sting. Many of us started to wonder whether, at least in part, we had been part of the First Church of Leopards Eating People's Faces. I remembered what one of those "liberal" exiles from the days of what people called "the Controversy" had said to me in my early twenties, when I was still a doctoral student. "You think that they are able to do all of this because of biblical conviction," he said. "One day you will see that it's really about power and career advancement and opportunism. You think that these people are a community for you, but you will find that the second you are no longer useful to them, they will do the same thing to you that they are now doing to us." I thought, "Well, of course a liberal would say that." There came a day, though, when I would be accused of being "the liberal"—without having changed my theology at all. I found that some of those I thought were wrong about the Bible and wrong about the gospel were right about us. And that was unsettling. I also started to realize that some of those "liberals" of the past really didn't disagree with me on the fundamental issues of whether the Bible errs or not or whether faith in Christ is necessary for salvation (although many, to be sure, did). I wondered, though, how many of even those outside those boundaries weren't exiled by their theological liberalism as much as they became theological liberals as a result of their exile. Maybe, I wondered, they rejected conservatism when they saw that what the powers that be were conserving was their own chauffeured cars and offering-funded expense accounts.

Discussing his own Republican Party and conservative political movement, David Frum described the vertigo of finding people who had been allies for years no longer speaking to him. Calling it a "process of estrangement," he explains it this way: "'I thought we believed X,' says the dissident. 'You're a bunch of hypocrites for now saying Y. You're betraying everything I thought we believed.' 'No,' reply the majority. 'We always deep down believed that Y was more important than X. We never before had to choose. Now we do. And if you choose X over Y, it's you who are betraying us.'" Frum writes that this is what economists call "revealed preference," which he defines as "a choice between two competing alternatives that forces the chooser to discover his highest values," often with the accompanying confusion of seeing "how radically their highest values differed from those of old allies and former comrades."* Many, seeing what people they thought were on their "side" could affirm, were left wondering, "Is this really what I signed up for?"

One of those moments, among many, for me, was hearing people in my "tribe" not simply arguing against the necessity of Christian character but making the point that a lack of Christian character is actually a benefit. One evangelical pastor said that the threats were so great that he didn't care about a president's "tone or vocabulary."

---

*David Frum, "What Never-Trumpers Want Now," *The Atlantic*, September 13, 2021.

Instead, he said, "I want the meanest, toughest, son of a you-know-what I can find." An ongoing message to Americans generally, and to evangelical Christians specifically, is that there is a vulnerability for us so great that it requires a suspension of civility and norms for the sake of fighting. As Donald Trump said to the "Stop the Steal" rally that later erupted into an attack on the United States Capitol, "If you don't fight, you won't have a country anymore." This attitude is channeled through and accelerated by Christian media. Not long ago, I watched two Christian political commentators arguing that their cultural opponents were so sinful as to have sunk to the level of the subhuman. "This is demonic. Our enemies are demonic," one said. "There's no turning the other cheek; there's no being winsome."

When I asked a friend, a keen analyst of American culture, why we have devolved into the cruelty and craziness of the present moment, he suggested it was because of a loss of a sense of sin, replacing it with a nonjudgmental sense of self-esteem and personal authenticity. I'm not sure I agree. It's not that we have moved into a time of a utopian sense of the goodness of human nature (although that would be bad enough). We don't deny human depravity; we take reassurance from it. We sense that everyone is really just about power and appetite, and therefore only those who guard their power and feed their appetites can survive. "You can't judge me; I'm a good person!" is replaced with "You can't judge me; you're a bad person too!"

What we have at the moment is not so much a prosperity gospel as a depravity gospel. And appeals to character or moral norms are met not with claims of "not guilty!" but with dismissals of "get real!" This is the kind of argument we've taken on without even noticing we've done so. I hear this line of argument all the time now—including sometimes applying it to sexually predatory ministers of the gospel. "Well, nobody's perfect; all are sinners; remember King David" can be used to defend the indefensible. Such an argument, when applied to the ministry, nullifies the biblical character qualifications of 1 Timothy 2–3 and elsewhere. And, when applied to oneself, can justify literally anything. "Even if I embezzle a little from my company, we're all sinners." "I cheat on my spouse a little, but Jesus said lust is adultery of the heart, so who hasn't?" This is precisely the kind of argument the Bible says is a contradiction of the gospel itself (Rom. 3:1–8).

That leads to a kind of "whataboutism" that contends that immorality is necessary to combat even worse immorality. The moral relativists become moral absolutists in a moment, and vice versa, and then flip back again. As one segregationist church elder in Jim Crow–era Birmingham reportedly said: "To hell with Christian principles—we've got to save the church!"* When a question of morality becomes "But what about the other side?," it doesn't matter where one stands on the religious or political or ideological spectrum—one has embraced a moral relativism that would make

---

*S. Jonathan Bass, *Blessed Are the Peacemakers: Martin Luther King Jr., Eight White Religious Leaders and the "Letter from Birmingham Jail"* (Baton Rouge: Louisiana State University Press, 2021), 86.

a postmodernist deconstructionist slink out of his faculty lounge in shame. When conscience means nothing, all that is left is power. The result is a nihilism that, history has shown us, ends up nowhere good.

Those of us who believe in what some call "total depravity" mean by that term that there's no part of a human being that isn't affected by sin. We can't find a part of us—our mind or our emotions or our will—that's sinless. We are, then, in need of repentance and mercy—as whole persons. What the doctrine does not mean is that everyone is as bad as they can possibly be, and therefore one cannot expect anything different. That's why the Scriptures include, for instance, character qualifications for gospel ministry (1 Tim. 2–3). Maybe the problem is not that we are a people obsessed with self-esteem, but instead that we are a people who've given up on esteeming anything or anyone. Maybe it's not just that we've neglected character formation, but that we don't think good character is possible at all. Maybe we've stopped pursuing holiness because we think that since everything's lost, nothing can be found; since everyone's blind, no one can see.

This collision of a state-of-the-emergency catastrophism with a "get real" depravity gospel ends up here. And here is not what we think it is. Our primary problem in this moral crisis is not that American evangelicals are hypocrites. Hypocrisy is always a problem against which the church must contend and in every era is a stumbling block to some people in believing the gospel. What we are seeing now, though, is in many cases the shucking off of even the pretense of hypocrisy for the outright embrace of immorality. Jerry Falwell Jr., the chancellor of the largest evangelical university in the country, was taken down by, among other things, allegations from a former pool boy that he benefited financially after agreeing to have sex with Falwell's wife while the Religious Right leader watched. This was a particularly salacious scandal, but not unheard of in the history of religious institutions. What was different, though, was that, after being caught, Falwell's defense was that he never claimed to be religious. He was a businessman, he said, and a lawyer, not a preacher.* The argument should have sounded familiar to those who paid attention to the justifications Falwell and others had made all along for Trump. We were not electing a pastor, they told us. He was a businessman, a tough guy who knew how to fight in the real world. It turns out, in the fullness of time, that this was the exact same argument that Falwell would make about himself.

When some of the details of the final days of the Falwell Jr. era were revealed, lots of people said, "How could he be this stupid and self-destructive?" But I don't think many of them said, "How could this happen? He was such a godly man." Falwell Jr. did not speak often in terms of the gospel or the way of Christ, even parenthetically, but in terms of decidedly Machiavellian political aims and objectives—often dismissing those who questioned the cost to Christian witness of merging evangelicalism with populist demagoguery

---

*Gabriel Sherman, "Son of a Preacher Man," *Vanity Fair*, March 2022.

as though they were morally preening puritans, out of touch with the real world. When confronted with the immorality and scandals of his preferred presidential candidate, Falwell didn't seek to measure the moral deficiencies with what he saw as the greater good as much as he ridiculed the premise of the question. Trump was moral because he had created jobs and made payroll. Unlike some other Trump evangelical supporters—with whom I disagreed but whose positions were reasonable and understandable—Falwell didn't try to measure the business leader's intemperate and crass attacks on people with some other objective—judicial nominations, for instance. Instead, he often mimicked such attacks, right along with the cartoonish and bullying tone of them. When his own scandals started to proliferate, Falwell did not defend himself as a faithful follower of Jesus Christ. He didn't even, as do so many scandal-ridden Christian leaders, present himself as a repentant David in the middle of Psalm 51. He said that he was a lawyer, not a preacher—as though the commands to integrity, obedience, repentance, and mercy were ordination vows instead of the call of Jesus on every one of his disciples and, even before that, written by God on the consciences of every human being.

What we have seen, often, whether publicly or sometimes secretly by boards to whom some Christian leaders are accountable, is the disconnection of personal virtue or character from achieving the goals of "winning" in the social arena, whether in politics or in the corporate mission of a church or a ministry. Perhaps this was forecast in an American context by something as small as the use of language. "Morality" or "virtue" came to be replaced in public messaging within the political activist wings of Christianity with "values." Religious conservatives were called "values voters," and groups crafted campaigns with slogans such as "I Vote Values." Even the caucus of members of Congress devoted to issues of concern to religious conservatives is called a "Values Action Team." To some degree, this was, no doubt, an attempt at better messaging to the public—"morality" can bring forth images of scarlet letter–branding Puritan parsons while "values" suggests what all the families at the children's Saturday morning soccer game hold in common. But maybe the language shift was more revealing than that. After all, "values" situates the primary meaning of morality in terms of what a community finds "valuable" rather than in a standard above and outside of the community.

What was waved away as matters of personal character turned out to have institutional implications. Every institution seems to be riven by heresy trials, creating their own accidental exiles, and expending their own trust with those to whom they were accountable. And almost every institution seems to be defining character by success rather than the other way around. Conservative scholar Yuval Levin maps out that institutions are meant to do more than just carry out a task. Institutions are meant to shape and form character. When any kind of institution fails—again, not in the sense of mere ineffectiveness but in the sense of maintaining integrity and credibility—the institution sets off a cycle. The institutions must be led by people with well-formed character, and that character is meant to be formed by institutions.* That made sense to me as an evangelical Christian, where I had been taught that personal character, which in the case of the church was to be rooted in the gospel and cultivated by the Holy Spirit and by the discipleship of the church, was necessary not just for the individual to be holy, but for the church itself. As the apostle Paul wrote to a church with a scandalously sinning member: "Don't you know that a little yeast leavens the whole batch of dough?" (1 Cor. 5:6 NIV) And, likewise, the Bible told us, the church as a community was to shape and form the integrity of its members (Eph. 4:11–16). It is no surprise that failing institutions produced rootlessness, loneliness, graft, resentment, and rage. And it was no surprise that people for whom rootlessness, loneliness, graft, resentment, and rage had been normalized would lead institutions to further ruin.

The wreckage of all this creates much more of it. Sociologist Brian Klaas notes that, in almost every endeavor, a disproportionate number of leaders displays what's called the "dark triad" of narcissism, psychopathy, and Machiavellianism. The problem is not so much that power corrupts, he argues, but that corruptible people seek power in the first place and that, maybe even more importantly, they don't give up. Using the example of despots such as Saddam Hussein, Muammar Gaddafi, and others, Klaas notes how

---

*Yuval Levin, *A Time to Build: From Family and Community to Congress and the Campus, How Recommitting to Our Institutions Can Revive the American Dream* (New York: Basic Books, 2020), 32.

dangerous it is to be a dictator—notice how many end up exiled or decapitated or torn to pieces by mobs of their own people. "So here's the question," Klaas asks, "Who looks at that job and thinks, 'I want to try that!'" The answer is, he argues, narcissists and psychopaths and Machiavellian power seekers.* They are the ones who think they are special enough to survive the onslaughts that will come. Or they are the ones with the psychological numbness not to care. Almost every day I have conversations with people on the verge of quitting, often pastors of local churches of all sizes and sometimes members of Congress. Their reasons are almost always the same. The congressperson ran for office because she wanted to contribute in serving people by making policy, but found herself in an institution where others ran in order to appear on cable news. The pastor went into ministry to teach the Bible and to care for the hurting; now he's shouted down over politics and conspiracy theories. As these people leave, guess who are left who don't mind such a toxic environment or who actually *like* it? Sociopaths.

What those who don't feel shame have learned is that, eventually, most people will be exhausted and "move on" and that one's hard-core "base" will learn to normalize whatever the character flaw is. If Billy Graham or Mother Teresa had been found to be using donor money to purchase private luxury jets, the scandal would have been in the first paragraph of their obituaries. On the other

---

*Brian Klaas, *Incorruptible: Who Gets Power and How It Changes Us* (New York: Simon & Schuster, 2021), 101.

hand, prosperity gospel evangelist Kenneth Copeland muses that he doesn't know why people criticize his private jets, since he doesn't know how a preacher is supposed to do his devotions while flying commercial. In that case, people shrug and think nothing more of it. In a performative age, brazenness gives an illusion of strength. After all, to apologize or to repent is to look weak. And when what people expect of their leaders is that they be avatars of vicarious power, weakness is the only unforgivable sin. In such an environment, by sheer Darwinian measures, the shameless are always going to have an advantage. If a lack of shame is what it takes to succeed, then sociopaths will proliferate. This means not only leaders without character but also followers who come to see character as itself a lack of the strength needed to fight whomever one deems one's enemies. Those who will shamelessly employ internet-troll tactics—whether on the actual internet or in church congregational or denominational meetings—have an advantage over those who would feel shame if they were to employ falsehood or rancor or what the Bible calls "an unhealthy craving for controversy" (1 Tim. 6:4). Those who can still feel shame, whose consciences are still vulnerable to conviction by the Holy Spirit, will then step back or step away, and the shameless will inherit, if not the earth, then at least the political party leadership or the congregation or the school board or the social media feed.

But, of course, shame never really goes anywhere but underground. Those who can't feel it still bear it. They find fig leaves to cover it, even as they project their shame elsewhere (Gen. 3:7–13).

Behind those quivering bushes, there are men and women scared of the presence of God—a fear they can easily translate into hostility toward those less shameless (Gen. 4:5–8) or boasting in their shameless dominance over those still weak enough to feel shame (Gen. 4:23–24). And so we end up concealing shame with more shamelessness, the lack of character with more cruelty, and with the very sorts of people the Bible commands us *not* to put in leadership. And so the cycle continues. Disintegrated persons lead to disintegrated institutions, and disintegrated institutions lead to disintegrated persons.

The Bible describes the human heart as "deceitful above all things, and desperately wicked: who can know it?" (Jer. 17:9 KJV) and also speaks of evil as "the mystery of iniquity" (2 Thess. 2:7 KJV). But what stands out to me in all these cases is something I've seen repeatedly in this quarter century of ministry, though usually with much lower stakes, and that's what modern psychology would call "projection." Projection, in short, is the idea that something loathed within oneself is then projected onto something or someone else, and then attacked ruthlessly. The philosopher Rene Girard devoted much attention to what he called a "scapegoat mechanism." According to Girard, groups form rivalries, because of common and imitated desires, and those rivalries seek an escape valve in the identifying of an agreed-upon object of hatred, the scapegoat, temporarily alleviating the conflict. This is not the same thing as "projection," by any means, but both see internal problems made external—with innocent people facing the brunt of the violence (whether physical, emotional, or spiritual). Cain perceived an injustice, that he felt as an insult, but directed his rage not at the invisible and invulnerable God but at his innocent brother in front of him. Thus, the apostle John equates the spirit of murder at work in Cain with those who say they love God but hate their brothers and sisters (1 John 3:11–18). And when found in murder, Cain's immediate thought goes to potential murderers out there who might seek to do to *him* what he did to his brother (Gen. 4:14).

The apostle Paul points out what some might today call "projection" in his letter to the church at Rome. After detailing the sins of the pagan world outside of the people of God (Rom. 1:18–2:16), noting that God's revelation in creation and conscience render everyone "without excuse," Paul turns what he expects to be nodding heads of judgment around on the readers themselves: ". . . you then who teach others, do you not teach yourself?" he writes. "While you preach against stealing, do you steal? You who say that one must not commit adultery, do you commit adultery? You who abhor idols, do you rob temples?" (Rom. 2:21–22). The point here is not only that the religious people—those entrusted to teach the Law— were *hypocrites* (although that's certainly true) but that they were accusing others of doing the *very things* they were guilty of doing. Indeed, we see that at work even among Jesus' original disciples— with Judas accusing a woman of wasting money that should go to the poor (John 12:4–5). Interestingly, John writes: "He said this, not because he cared about the poor, but because he was a thief, and having charge of the moneybag he used to help himself to what was put into it" (John 12:6). Note that John did not write that Judas said this *even though* he was a thief but *because* he was a thief.

The problem was not just that he was a hypocrite, but that he was accusing an innocent third party of *the very thing he was doing at the time.* Indeed, in Mark's account of the story, the disciples who accused this woman (leaving Judas unnamed here) "said to themselves indignantly, 'Why was the ointment wasted like that?'" (Mark 14:4). They said *to themselves*, the Bible says, and they said this not with the appearance of being indignant but with the reality of it. The problem was not just the deception of others, but the deception of self. Thus, some people who devote their lives purportedly to the objectivity of truth turn to the subjectivity of truth when telling vulnerable women that they are "helping the ministry" by their being abused. And some who loathe themselves for their immorality turn their rage against those innocent people they deem "temptations" rather than seeing where the guilt and shame really resides—within themselves.

I've seen over and over again people who cover their own internal shame and guilt with a seeming mission to shame others for the very things to which they are secretly in bondage. This is not irony or coincidence; it is a key aspect of how depravity works. That's why the Bible speaks of "the mind that is set on the flesh" (Rom. 8:6–7) both in terms of sexual anarchy *and* envy *and* violence *and* quarrelsomeness *and* religious zeal apart from the gospel (Gal. 5:13–21; Phil. 3:3–11). The very act of denunciation can *feel* like discipleship— at least for a moment. But it destroys the person doing this—and often innocent others too. Some of the most ferocious of denounc-ers of sexual immorality "in the culture" are sexual nihilists inside. Some of the most virulent defenders of orthodoxy have psyches de-void of prayer. But, like the priests of Baal shrieking and cutting themselves, they do so not because they believe so much but, rather, because they really believe in nothing. That's too terrifying a reality to face so they find other dragons to fight. For some, a culture war is the price to be paid in order to feel Christian, when there's noth-ing genuine inside—except shame and guilt and fear and loneliness. "It is the magician's bargain: give up our soul, get power in return," C. S. Lewis wrote. "But once our souls, that is, ourselves, have been given up, the power thus conferred will not belong to us. We shall in fact be the slaves and puppets of that to which we have given our souls."*

So, if you want a different path forward, what should you do?

Prioritize Long-Term Integrity Over Short-Term Success. Are the moral compromises described here worth it in order to have influ-ence in a culture war? Only if social conformity to a set of rules is more important than a person's conscience before the Judgment Seat of Christ. And yet, even on its own terms, this sort of demor-alized religion does not work. Look, for instance, at Ireland, once culturally ruled by the Roman Catholic Church, an outlier in the rest of Europe when it came to abortion laws and even divorce. All that is reversed now. Did these massive and unpredictably sudden

*C. S. Lewis, *The Abolition of Man* (New York: HarperCollins, 1944), 75–76.

changes happen because of dramatically improved mobilization or messaging tactics by the (to use an American framing) "cultural Left"? No. Many researchers believe that the cultural shifts in Ireland were due, in large part, to a backlash against the church itself. Was this backlash because of cultural forces of secularization warring against the church? No. It was because people who once revered the church came to believe that the church did not itself believe what it taught. When the church's cover-up of sexual abuse, in a horrifying broad and systemic way, was brought to light, the nation saw, writes historian Fintan O'Toole, that the church's influence had been so great as to disable a society's ability to know right from wrong, apart from the institution's say-so. This was to the extent that, in some instances, parents were actually apologizing to the priests who molested their children. When people began to see what had happened, they came to what O'Toole calls "the most shocking realization of all," namely, "the recognition by most of the faithful that they were in fact much holier than their preachers, that they had a clearer sense of right and wrong, a more honest and intimate sense of love and compassion and decency."* The result, perhaps for born-again America, as for Catholic Ireland, is an inordinately powerful force of cultural influence, if not moral authority, that finds itself suddenly without the credibility to enforce its orthodoxies at all, even with its own children.

---

*Fintan O'Toole, *We Don't Know Ourselves: A Personal History of Modern Ireland* (New York: W. W. Norton, 2021), 567.

Most of the cultural projects in American history that one can imagine that were undertaken from a posture of Christian strength and influence (Prohibition, for instance) have failed. Two causes in particular—the struggle for religious liberty for all in the founding era and the civil rights movement—succeeded with Christian movements that were on the cultural margins of influence. In the first, Baptists, and the second, the Black church. In both of these cases, a lack of cultural power actually helped their message be heard rather than hindering it. Baptists were disreputable enough in Anglican America that reasonable people ultimately did not see disestablishment of a state church as a stalking horse for Baptist power—first of all because this, in fact, was not their motive and, second, because few could imagine "Baptist power" anyway. The civil rights movement modeled nonviolence and a persuasive appeal to conscience. Structural power and legal power were needed, of course, to pass and enforce and interpret the resulting (and essential) legislation, but such could only happen because people without what we would call "influence" spoke with credibility. When sharecropper Fannie Lou Hamer said to the white-supremacist Mississippi power structure around her, "Do you people think about when you'll have to meet God?," she could do so only because she believed it, she was right, and she was willing to live a life that demonstrated it.* The same can be true for you in your sphere of life.

---

*Charles Marsh, *God's Long Summer: Stories of Faith and Civil Rights* (Princeton: Princeton University Press, 2008), 23.

In a context of performativity, "fighting" can feel to some people almost like morality—it's a matter of signing up with the "moral" side and blasting the "immoral" side. One can even start to measure one's morality by the extent of the "fight," and by having "all the right enemies." But even assuming you are right in your "moral positions," is that really the case? Why does the Bible call for church leaders to be "well thought of by outsiders" (1 Tim. 3:7)? The apostle Peter wrote, "Keep your conduct among the Gentiles [the outsiders] honorable, so that when they speak against you as evildoers, they may see your good deeds and glorify God on the day of visitation" (1 Pet. 2:12). Your neighbors—even your very secular "None" neighbors—probably do not hate you as much as you've been led to think. But even when they *do*, Peter wrote that if we are slandered it should not be because of our evil-doing but because of what the Bible defines as "good" (1 Pet. 3:13–17). And that good includes speaking to outsiders "with gentleness and respect" as we bear witness to Christ and while having "a good conscience" (1 Pet. 3:15–16). What matters is not just what happens to "the culture," but what happens to *you*. If you commend what is evil because it's the best way to fight what you find more evil, all we end up with is a haggling contest over the price of one's soul.

Pay Attention to Means, Not Just to Ends. As you think through your own witness, consider what's really going on when a great deal of what now passes for evangelical Christianity says that "turn the other cheek" and "winsomeness" won't work. The argument is often that such things are fine for a "neutral culture," but not in this, a "hostile culture." Never mind that the Sermon on the Mount was not delivered in Mayberry, but in Roman-occupied territory. Crucifixion seems hostile. When the centurions of the biblical story start to look more valiant to us than the crucified, then maybe our culture wars have taken us away from the cross and toward something else. If the American church thinks "turn the other cheek" is surrender and weakness, then wait until they hear "take up your cross and follow me."

The idea of a culture neutral to Christianity is itself a liberalizing religion. The Bible tells us that people, from Eden on, are not divided into those hostile to the gospel and those not. The apostle Paul writes: "None is righteous, no, not one; no one understands; no one seeks for God" (Rom. 3:10–11). Hostility to God can show itself as felt hatred of God, but can, even more perniciously, show itself as the attempt to use God or "Christianity" for one's own gain and goals (Acts 8:18–23). To think that pretend Christianity—claiming the goals of Jesus while ditching his ways; a culture embracing Christian values without individual new birth—is somehow closer to Christ than is outright paganism is the opposite of what Jesus himself told us (Matt. 21:31).

In recent years, it has become popular—especially among a certain kind of fundamentalist Calvinist on social media—to mock the idea of "winsomeness" in Christian witness. As I was writing this page, one figure did so, attacking a revered elder evangelical, as he was in the hospital being treated for terminal cancer. The point was that "winsomeness" doesn't work in these times. Now, the argument goes, the only effective measure is a gloves-off "fighting" evangelicalism, of the sarcastic and condemnatory sort. The idea is that this figure—and those who similarly seek to treat outsiders with respect and gentleness—does so because it "works." Almost no consideration is given to the fact that perhaps what is being sought is not "winsomeness" as a strategy but the following of *Christ*. The commands to "gentleness" and "reasonableness" as well as that a person crucify "quarrelsomeness" and a "craving for controversy" are on almost every page of the New Testament.

Does that "work"? This is the equivalent of saying that sexual chastity doesn't "work" in a time of decreased population pressure because a faithful marriage can't impregnate as many women as orgies. Is that true? Yes. Does that matter? No. The outcome is not the measure of the morality—obedience to the way of Christ is, and the loss of one's own character is not worth any real or imagined outcome. In one sense, you will indeed be at a disadvantage if you opt for Christlikeness. But it's the same sort of disadvantage that "normal" people at a family reunion have who do not brandish firearms and turn over the furniture to win an argument. Yes, the ones shooting through the sheetrock and screaming profanities will probably "get the last word," but do you want to trade places with them? No. Would your conclusion be, "Next year, we are really going to need more cocaine and weaponry of our own, if we're going to be heard"? No. You would say, "This is dysfunctional. We will be elsewhere during the reunion dinner next year, and, as a matter of fact, we're leaving now."

Sometimes we must be ready to "speak a word" into a controversy, but often what is called for is for someone to model the different way of valuing his or her own soul over having something to say. When it comes to those for whom quarreling is a way of life, the way to win is not to win at their game but to play a different game altogether. If you conform to Christ only when the culture is "neutral" enough to allow you to win on their terms, then Jesus is not Lord and you are not his disciple. You are Lord and he is your disciple. Just as culture-warring is easier than conversion, influence is easier than integrity.

The late pastor Eugene Peterson, in a letter to his son, also a pastor, wrote that the primary problem for the Christian leader is to take responsibility not just for the ends but also for the "ways and means" by which we guide people to pursue those ends. "The devil's three temptations of Jesus all had to do with ways and means," he wrote. "Every one of the devil's goals was excellent. The devil had an unsurpassed vision statement. But the ways and means were incompatible with the ends."* As Peterson put it, the discipleship that Jesus calls us to is one "both personally and corporately conducted in which the insides and outsides are continuous. A life in which we are as careful and attentive to the *how* as to the *what*."

---

*Eric E. Peterson and Eugene H. Peterson, *Letters to a Young Pastor: Timothy Conversations Between Father and Son* (Colorado Springs: NavPress, 2020), 140.

This is because, Peterson counseled, "if we are going to live the Jesus life, we simply have to do it the Jesus way—he is, after all, the Way as well as the Truth and Life."* There are no emergency escape clauses from the way of the cross.

Expect Better from Institutions (Especially the Church). Remember the lure of the depravity gospel. It doesn't matter if you get to it by adopting it outright, with glee at cruelty and vulgarity, or if it drives you to the kind of cynicism that doesn't ever expect anything better. That way lies nihilism. You will find yourself in situations, and you may be in one of those situations already, where you have a responsibility for holding an institution accountable. Maybe it's simply as a voter. You can just shrug and give your assent to anyone your party tells you to support. That will change you, over time. Maybe it's as a church member or a part of some denomination or Christian ministry. Do not confuse giftedness with character, in yourself or in anyone else. You shouldn't expect your leaders to be sinless. They will sin, but there's a difference between a sinning, repenting human being and a pattern of corruption. If the latter, you will have to ask yourself how to address it. Is it through staying where you are and seeking to effect change? Or is it by leaving and finding a new place to live and to serve? I don't know. Much of that is contingent on factors you often just can't know. I would suggest that you ask yourself where your vulnerabilities are. Are you the kind of person who normally defaults to leaving a situation? If so,

---

*Ibid., 98–99.

---

then find all the reasons you should stay and make change, before you leave. Are you the kind of person who tends to just adapt yourself to a situation, out of obligation or loyalty or nostalgia? If so, strongly consider leaving. The accountability of our institutions matters. They are what norm us into what we consider to be "normal." When awful behavior starts to feel normal to you, it's not just you who are in danger.

Protect Your Own Conscience. A conscience is more than just an internal prompter saying "Do the right thing." Conscience is a way of knowing—like reason and imagination and intuition—that is embedded deep in the human psyche. Conscience alerts us to the fact that we live in a morally structured cosmos, and that our lives exist in a timeline that is moving us toward a day of accountability (Rom. 2:15–16), a Judgment Seat before one who endured, for us, his own judgment seat (John 19:13). What that does is to equip a person to have a long-term view of the universe, and of one's own life. With a short-term view (of, say, a hundred years or so), one could easily conclude that *ambition* is the driver of life. One could conclude, as does the Psalmist and Job, that the ruthless prosper, and that therefore the way to prosperity is through ruthlessness. Conscience, when functioning well, points a person to a broader scope—toward the day when everything is brought to accountability, and one's life really begins.

That starts with being rather than doing. That's precisely what evangelical movements of all sorts emphasize. "For by grace you have been saved through faith. And this is not your own doing; it is the gift of God, not a result of works, so that no one may boast" (Eph. 2:8–9). This is immediately followed with this: "For we are his workmanship, created in Christ Jesus for good works, which God prepared beforehand, that we should walk in them" (Eph. 2:10). The morality is important but morality is rooted in life, not the other way around. If you are in Christ, your sins are forgiven. You are crucified with Christ, and raised with him. There is nothing to earn. That's why, at its best, evangelical Christianity has pointed to morality—or, in better biblical language, sanctification—as an out-working of who we already are in Christ, not as a way to earn favor with God. Morality, then, is opposed to *moralism* or *legalism*. As Martin Luther put it, "We do not become righteous by doing righteous deeds but, having been made righteous, we do righteous deeds."*

Morality must be something defined outside of the person and outside of the situation. The cross is a definitive judgment against objectively defined sin. So is hell. Sin has to do not just with *what you are doing* (although it certainly includes that) but also with *what kind of person you are becoming.* We have different points of vulnerability, which is why we have to bear one another's burdens. Watch in your own life where those weak points are. What is the ambition that drives you? Who are the people you want to like you? A nonfunctioning conscience is informed by the priorities of

---

*Martin Luther, "Disputation Against Scholastic Theology," in *Martin Luther's Basic Theological Writings*, ed. Timothy F. Lull (Minneapolis: Fortress, 1989), 16.

ambition and safety and belonging. That's how Pontius Pilate ended up a crucifier of Jesus. It's not because he was plotting to see this Messiah killed, but because he was "wishing to satisfy the crowd" (Mark 15:15). Pilate, Matthew writes, "saw that he was gaining nothing, but rather that a riot was beginning," and so he washed his hands of the matter (Matt. 27:24). That's how it happens. Pilate saw the stakes as being about what he was gaining or losing—in that moment, or in the sweep of his life. He defined his mission in terms of ambition and security rather than in terms of conscience. And so his conscience adjusted to his ambition, not the other way around. The same can happen to you—no matter if you work in a grocery store produce department or in an accounting firm or in a screenwriting guild or as a missionary. The pull will always be to quiet the conscience because you can't afford what you fear it may ask of you. In that direction lies disaster. The problem is not that you will find yourself moving in ways you never wanted to move—but, rather, that you will not notice at all how you are moving. You will not even see that you are chasing the imprimatur of whatever crowd to which you want to belong, to whatever goal you want to achieve, until only after it is too late do you see that you no longer recognize yourself. That clamor for ambition and belonging will lead not to an absence of conscience but to a misdirected conscience, one that feels shame about what is not shameful, and feels nothing about what is.

Character formation works from the inside out too. Jesus said,

"The good person out of the good treasure of his heart produces good, and the evil person out of his evil treasure produces evil, for out of the abundance of the heart his mouth speaks" (Luke 6:45).

A clear conscience does not lead, as we imagine, to inner tranquility, at least not right away. A clear conscience is a conscience that is alive—and thus is vibrating with prompts to repentance and redirection and pleas for mercy. But, in the long run, a clear conscience leads to peace—because it casts out fear. If your ambition is your standard, you are enslaved to whatever can take away your ambition. If your belonging in your tribe is your standard, then you will be terrified at any threat of exile. But if your mission lines up with your conscience and your conscience lines up with the gospel, then you have no need to live in paralyzing fear, and you also have no need to live in defense of yourself. That's why Jesus told his disciples, "So have no fear of them, for nothing is covered that will not be revealed, or hidden that will not be known. What I tell you in the dark, say in the light, and what you hear whispered, proclaim on the housetops" (Matt. 10:26–27). If you are aware that there is a Judgment Day to come, you do not need to call your own judgment day now. And if anyone asks anything of you at the cost of your integrity, know that the price is too high.

Whatever the secular worlds around us may say about the relativity of morality and the nonexistence of such categories as "sin" and "judgment," no one really believes that. That's why among many people who are not Christians (sadly, right now, often more than among Christians), there is a passion for justice. There also are the pangs of conscience, when we've hurt someone, when we've betrayed our own integrity, that persist, no matter what abstractions one might believe. Flannery O'Connor once wrote about the burden of a guilty conscience in her own southern Catholic subculture, in which some are never sure whether their confessions are adequate or if they are "compounding sin on sin." She said this sort of scrupulosity probably comes from "being taught by the Sisters to measure your sins with a slide rule." That is not sustainable. "It drives some folks nuts and some folks to the Baptists," she wrote. "I felt sure it will drive me nuts and not to the Baptists."* Now, I can testify that these are not necessarily two different categories, but her larger point remains. The burden of a guilty conscience contributes to an awful lot of craziness. And it doesn't just happen in pre–Vatican II Catholic enclaves, like hers, or in strict evangelical settings either. Guilt and shame are universal human problems. And the desire sometimes to start over is also a universal human longing. The world needs to see moral consistency from those of us who claim to be "the saved." The way they see that consistency is not with a people who are without sins and injustices and flaws, but with a people who know how to *repent*.

---

*Flannery O'Connor, "To Father James H. McCown," letter dated January 12, 1958, in *Flannery O'Connor: Collected Works*, ed. Sally Fitzgerald (New York: Library of America, 1988), 1061.

The very first of the theses Martin Luther nailed to the cathedral door made the point: "When our Lord Jesus Christ said, 'Repent' (Matt. 4:17), he willed the entire life of believers to be one of repentance."* Few things could be more needed in a time in which "saving face" is one of the most important priorities, and in which "I'm sorry" is usually forced by social-media mobs threatening the loss of a job rather than from a sense of remorse for wrongdoing. There are all sorts of substitutes for repentance.

When talking with younger Christians, I almost never encounter people who want to justify their sins and deny the need for repentance as much as I encounter those who think they're failing, and that they're bad Christians. When I press, I find that these Christians usually are expecting to repent of a sin *one* time and then never grapple with it again. This is not how repentance works. Sometimes what they're expecting is a kind of "peace," a rest from the awareness of one's self as a sinner, a rest from the need to repent of sin. If that's you, what you are expecting is achievable, but you will have to be dead first. What you're expecting is to be something other than a sinner. That will happen, but when it does, you will be in the New Jerusalem in the presence of Christ. If you think you experience it before then, you are actually just finding a way to call

---

*Martin Luther, "Ninety-Five Theses, or, Disputation on the Power and Efficacy of Indulgences," in *Martin Luther's Basic Theological Writings*, ed. Timothy F. Lull (Minneapolis: Fortress, 1989), 21.

your sin something other than sin. And that's, well, sin. The ordinary Christian life involves the kind of spiritual warfare Jesus taught us to wage—which starts with "Our Father" and continues through "Forgive us of our trespasses" all the way through "Deliver us from evil." You will never get too spiritually "successful" to move to some other way of praying. You "win" by confessing your sins, claiming the gospel that tells you there is no condemnation for those who are in Christ (Rom. 8:1).

Forgiveness is not rooted in the absence of judgment but in the presence of it. "Judge not," Jesus said, not because "who's to say what's wrong or right?" We don't judge—in the sense that Jesus meant the term—precisely because *God does*, and because we know that we will stand before that same Judgment Seat. The idea that this should lead to a lack of accountability for sin and injustice—especially when done in the name of Jesus himself—is the opposite of the gospel of Jesus Christ. If "forgiveness" and "grace" allow those with power in the church to keep using that power to harm vulnerable people, then Jesus, with all the prophets and apostles, tells us that we have not understood the gospel (1 John 3:11–18). To do that is to turn the best news in the cosmos into just one more Darwinian strategy for domination. The problem of the Corinthian church is ours right now. They were tempted to be *too judgmental* with the sins of the outside world and *not judgmental* enough with those on the inside (1 Cor. 5:12–13). It's always easier to do the reverse, because that's self-protection, not integrity.

The situation within this morally compromised American church is a scandal, and by "scandal" I don't mean our contemporary popular usage of the word, of the exposure of anything gossip-worthy. I mean it in its historic theological sense—as a lack of integrity by the people of God that serves as a "stumbling block" to the outside world seeing Christ for who he is, the gospel for what it is. You cannot give to others what you do not have. As the prophet Ezekiel was told to dramatically enact carrying "exile's baggage" as a way of showing Israel their coming judgment (Ezek. 12:1–16), maybe what the church is most called to do in this moment is not, first, to preach repentance but to embody what repentance looks like so that a culture seeking forgiveness will know what the words even mean. That's a matter of our moral credibility and of our gospel clarity too. That can't happen if our standard of morality is this twisted. That can't happen if we are the moral relativists we warned about. If morality means everything, no gospel is necessary, but if morality means nothing, no gospel is true.

CHAPTER FIVE

LOSING OUR
STABILITY

How Revival Can Save Us
from Nostalgia

Willie Nelson was a door-to-door Bible salesman, but that didn't work out. Then he tried to find his way as a country music singer, but that didn't work out either. He tried for years to fit the image and sound of what Music Row executives and national radio audiences expected from country music, until he gave up on pleasing Nashville and moved back to Texas. One friend said: "You get the impression that when he was living in Nashville he was sending out his songs like a stranded man sends out messages in bottles, and that when he moved to Austin, he suddenly discovered that all those bottles had floated to shore among friends."* As historians of the era described it, "Back

---

*Dayton Duncan and Ken Burns, *Country Music: An Illustrated History* (New York: Knopf, 2019), 348.

in his native Texas, Nelson started over—and revived his career."* At the same time, a similar revival was happening in the lives of some other singer-songwriters, in what came to be known as "outlaw country."

Outlaw country was so named not because it deals lyrically with bandits and thieves (although, naturally, it sometimes does) but because it started well outside of the cultural norms of the Nashville establishment. As one observer put it, "They resisted the music industry's unwritten rules, which prescribed the length, the meter, and the lyrical content of the songs as well as how those songs were recorded in the studio."† But more than just the craft of the music itself, these renegades dissented against the expected cultural look and feel of country music. "Rhinestone suits and new shiny cars, we've done the same thing for years," Waylon Jennings plaintively sang. "We need to change."‡ At the time, the industry seemed to have the winning argument. In order to reach emerging markets, they reasoned, country music must sound more like the music Americans liked. The formula worked. The outlaws asked, referring to the legend Hank Williams, "Are You Sure Hank Done It

---

*Ibid.

†Michael Streissguth, *Outlaw: Waylon, Willie, Kris, and the Renegades of Nashville* (New York: William Morrow, 2014), 2.

‡Waylon Jennings, "Are You Sure Hank Done It This Way," lyrics, copyright: RCA, 1975.

This Way?" but they lost the argument; the market knew what it wanted and the executives knew how to give it to them.

In their exile from Music Row, the outlaws were able, at last, to write the songs that seemed real to them. Turns out, they seemed real to others too. And, before long, steel guitars and bandanas would supplement, if not wholly replace, rhinestones and hairspray. Ironically enough, the outlaws were not dissidents because they rejected country music tradition but because they loved it. They were, in the words of one journalist, "about the only folks in Nashville who will walk into a room where there's a guitar and a *Wall Street Journal* and pick up the guitar."* Also ironic is the fact that the outlaws and their allies, with their songs that were dismissed by executives as too gritty or too intellectual or even "too country," would turn out to be the ones who could bridge the cultural form into other markets, not just with the outlaws but with their fellow travelers and those they influenced. Rednecks and hippies both loved Johnny Cash.

The Nashville establishment was hardly wrong to wonder why they needed reform. They were, after all, selling records, making money. Kris Kristofferson writing songs based on Voltaire's *Candide* did not seem to be the future. "The Opry audience was the Nashville Sound's target demographic, and no one's ever eager to fix a cash machine that isn't broken," one journalist observed. "But

---

*Streissguth, *Outlaw*, 155.

threads wear, imperceptibly at first, before they rip."* That's true even for threads studded with rhinestones. The outlaw genre brought an infusion of change, without which the music form quite likely would have marketed its way into the very end it sought to avoid: a homogenous and aging cultural cul-de-sac with little relevance to those who were not already fans. That means, of course, the industry would have succeeded its way to oblivion. The art form required a revival of sorts, the kind of revival that needed at least a few outlaws to spur it along.

The outlaw experience is mirrored in many different art forms. Think of the development of jazz, which came to be, not in symphony halls but in tiny clubs in New Orleans and Harlem and Chicago. The same could be said of the blues in the Mississippi Delta to hip-hop pioneers on both coasts. Mozart might even be thought of as "outlaw classical." Marketing guru Seth Godin points to the Grateful Dead as an example within the rock music framework of what he calls appealing to the "smallest viable audience."† For Godin, the smallest viable audience principle isn't about keeping "authentic" by adopting a "small is beautiful" mindset. It's instead the realization that genuine change in art—and he defines "art" to mean any creative contribution to business, labor, and the crafts, as well

---

*Ryan White, *Jimmy Buffett: A Good Life All the Way* (New York: Touchstone, 2017), 75.

†Seth Godin, *This Is Marketing: You Can't Be Seen Until You Learn to See* (New York: Penguin Random House, 2018), 94–95.

as to what we typically think of as art—comes about not by finding the lowest common denominator of what the "market" is thought to expect but by mattering a great deal to a relative few. If the contribution is worthy, the few will find a sense of belonging in their shared experience of that art and it will spread and grow. Usually— as in the case of outlaw country and many of the other musical expressions listed above—the change happens not just with newness but also with a reconnection to the best aspects of the past. A revival of anything often looks disturbingly different or doomed to irrelevance but really is a reconnection to roots so old they now seem new.

In that, it seems to me, is both a parable and a warning for an American conservative Protestantism seeking revival—whether by "revival" we mean the mundane sense that these musicians meant it, a comeback, or in the larger, more supernatural meaning of the word. When many people think of evangelical Christianity, a form of revival imagery is the first thing that comes to mind. For some, that might be the brush arbors of the nineteenth century or the sawdust trail tent meetings of the early twentieth or the midcentury stadium crusades of Billy Graham and Luis Palau. Many others see in "revival" political overtones. They see purportedly evangelistic rallies that are about mobilizing voters, and they see political rallies in which soft music plays in the background at the end, as one almost expects the political figure to invite the crowd to walk forward to register to vote. Often when one hears an evangelical preacher thundering, "God send a revival!" or "We need awakening in this land!," what he or she means is "Let's win the culture war."

I find myself reluctant to use the word *revival* because the category serves for so many of my fellow American evangelical Christians as a kind of deus ex machina, a plot twist that suddenly reverses secularization or any of the crises currently facing the church. "Well, we're just going to have to pray for revival," one might say. When pressed, some of these people seem to expect a sudden turnaround to the status quo normal in religious life to whatever period of time they knew before. Revival, for them, means "getting back to normal," except with more people. History and demography seem to suggest otherwise. In a major study of American demographics, projecting major decline for Christianity, the demographers at Pew Research said that "there is no data on which to model a sudden or gradual revival of Christianity (or of religion in general) in the U.S." They wrote: "That does not mean a religious revival is impossible. It means there is no demographic basis on which to project one." A Bible-believing Christian would respond to such research by saying that it's rooted in antisupernaturalism, similar to a doctor telling a bone cancer patient that prayer will not help that person to heal. That's almost right. But wouldn't we want a physician at the very least to tell a patient that based on the normal trajectory, things do not look good? God can, and has, healed, but if the patient is abandoning chemotherapy to attend a faith healer's rallies, one would want the doctor to tell the patient the most likely scenario.

The bigger question, though, is whether we should want revival at all.

Trauma experts have shown that often the implications of trauma are not even conscious to the person bearing it. Often it's the nervous system that points the way—signaling that something's wrong through a variety of symptoms—sometimes long before the mind is ready to acknowledge that there might be a problem. I heard one trauma expert speak to this by noting that one of the most counterproductive measures one can take in recovering from trauma is to attempt to speed through the healing process. Often people want a checklist of the ways to recover from a horrible situation—including those of spiritual abuse or trauma—so they can "move on" quickly with their lives. The path to healing, though, she argues, is not so simple and usually requires a slower, more deliberate attempt at grounding—at sorting through what happened. That's important, she says, because, as she puts it, "What is not repaired is repeated."*

What is not repaired is repeated.

What the church has experienced, and inflicted, over the past several years could only be described as a collective trauma. We see the implications in the wrecked lives, the split churches, the compromised witness. If the body keeps the score, maybe the Body of Christ does too. If the church is a household, how do we know that what we've lived through is not, at least in some cases, similar to

---

*Quoted in Russell Moore, "The Body of Christ Keeps Score," *Christianity Today*, August 24, 2022.

the toxic family background from which many people we know have come? Over and over again, I have seen people assume that the situation they've survived is "normal," and they seem to find themselves in the scenarios over and over again, without ever detecting the warning signs. This doesn't just happen with families but also with churches and church movements. What is not repaired is repeated.

One Christian leader thought that maybe we should say no to revival. "A religion, even popular Christianity, could enjoy a boom altogether divorced from the transforming power of the Holy Spirit and so leave the church of the next generation worse off than it would have been if the boom had never occurred," he wrote. "I believe that the imperative need of the day is not simply revival, but a radical reformation that will go to the root of our moral and spiritual maladies and deal with causes rather than with consequences, with the disease rather than with the symptoms." He concluded, "It is my considered opinion that under the present circumstances we do not want revival at all. A widespread revival of the kind of Christianity we know today in America might prove to be a moral tragedy from which we would not recover in a hundred years."*

What's astounding is, first of all, *who* made this point—not a liberalizing dissident, and not a confessionally Reformed skeptic of

---

*A. W. Tozer, "No Revival Without Reformation," in *Keys to the Deeper Life* (Louisville: GLH Publishing, 1957), 2.

the "man-centeredness" of revivals. This was A. W. Tozer, one of the most widely read evangelical advocates of what was sometimes called a "deeper life spirituality." Countless evangelical Christians start their mornings reading meditations from Tozer, seeking from him direction on how to pray, how to be renewed in communion with God. What's also astounding is *when* this was written. It was not in the maelstrom of the post-Trump evangelical intramural divisions, nor was it after a series of scandals by television evangelists or traveling apologists. This was written in 1957, just a year after Billy Graham and Carl F. H. Henry founded *Christianity Today*, the year of Graham's New York crusade that filled Yankee Stadium with a reported eighty thousand persons and was said to be the largest religious event in American history to that point. What Tozer was warning about seems oddly similar to me to the much more modern idea of trauma repetition. If what we mean by "revival" is a resurgence of American Christianity—with all the numbers and influence and programs and reputation the church once had—the results could indeed be catastrophic. Jesus warned the religious leadership of his time: "Woe to you, scribes and Pharisees, hypocrites! For you travel across sea and land to make a single proselyte, and when he becomes a proselyte, you make him twice as much a child of hell as yourselves" (Matt. 23:15). Jesus' point—after laying bare the ways the religious leaders were lifelessly mimicking religion and exploiting the piety of their followers—was that "reviving" or expanding such lifelessness makes a terrible situation even worse.

Revival in the Scriptures is tied to the idea of resurrection. Not everything that is life-continuing is resurrection, though. Of this generation of white evangelicals, Robert P. Jones writes, "Their greatest temptation will be to wield what remaining political power they have as a desperate corrective for their waning cultural influence. If this happens, we may be in for another decade of close skirmishes in the culture wars, but white evangelical Protestants will mortgage their future to resurrect the past." The danger, he notes, is forgetting this: "Like Mary Shelley's Frankenstein, resurrection by human power rather than divine spirit always produces a monstrosity."* Indeed, the fiery sword of the angel is placed at the entrance of Eden, the Bible tells us, to "guard the way to the tree of life" precisely because God did not want a twisted, fallen humanity to live forever in that state of death (Gen. 3:24). An undying humanity without spiritual life is not resurrection life, after all, but a zombie story—the corruption and decay is animated and without endpoint, but still horrifically dead. Almost every high school student has read the short story "The Monkey's Paw," about a wish for a dead loved one to be brought back to life. The terror comes about because that person is indeed made alive but just as he is—a decomposing nightmare. As Jesus warned a first-century church, "You have the reputation of being alive, but you are dead" (Rev. 3:1).

Nostalgia is, in and of itself, not a bad thing. In fact, it can well be the kind of "homesickness" and longing that is a signpost of God's

*Robert P. Jones, *The End of White Christian America* (New York: Simon & Schuster, 2016), 231.

grace. What we call "nostalgia" can actually, though, be a desperation to get back to the past in ways that are dangerous, even deadly.
In "revival," many Americans fear that what evangelical Christians
really mean is "taking America back" to some era of the past, maybe
the 1950s, to which few women or minorities would want to return.
This is not an unreasonable concern. In the churn of American life
right now, and religious life particularly, the pull to nostalgia is
strong. One study showed that 71 percent of white American evangelicals said that the country has changed mostly for the worse
since the 1950s, compared with less than half of Black Protestants
and only 37 percent of the religiously unaffiliated.* Whether the
imagined golden age of the past was the 1950s or the 1980s or the
1850s or the 500s, a key word in "Make America Great Again" is
the "again," with the timing of the first greatness often left intentionally open to interpretation. This is consistent with Christian
nationalist and Religious Right rhetoric of the past half century: "Re-
claiming America for Christ" or "Bringing God Back to America."
Notice, for instance, the "Restoring Honor" rally on the National
Mall in Washington DC in 2010. The language of "revival" was used,
of America "turning back to God" as a result of that movement. The
"revival" was led by a Mormon shock jock talk-radio host, complete
with a "black-robed regiment" of evangelical leaders behind him,

---

*"Challenges in Moving Toward a More Inclusive Democracy: Findings from the
2022 American Values Survey," Public Religion Research Institute, October 27,
2022.

virtually all of whom would have said throughout their ministries that a Latter-day Saint doctrine of Christ or salvation is not consistent with the gospel. Now, they hailed "revival" and said that the talk-show host "sounds like Billy Graham."* He was a "baby Christian," I suppose. What was meant by "revival" here was not the articulation of the gospel, the presentation of Jesus as redeemer of the world, but opposing a Democratic president's health care and tax plans, which they said were an existential threat to the country. These health care and tax policies are still in place and not even mentioned by most of these leaders.

Just as with the pull of progressives toward more or less utopian views of the future, sometimes more traditionalist nostalgia is just that, a temperament shaped by the conservative tradition of skepticism toward change. But, as with the utopianism of the Left, this temperament can become violent. The so-called Great Replacement Theory is an example of the sort of conspiracy theory that can proliferate when longing for an idealized (and often imaginary) past is combined with anxiety about the future. Even when the nostalgia that drives us is not of this noxious sort (the kind that would wave the flags and erect the monuments of the Confederacy, for instance), it can still lead to what *New York Times* columnist Ross Douthat labels "decadence," a situation in which the old order is exhausted and played out, yet prevents anything new from form-

---

*Frances Fitzgerald, *The Evangelicals: The Struggle to Shape America* (New York: Simon & Schuster, 2017), 597–98.

ing.* In other words, as Waylon Jennings sang, "Lord, it's the same old tune, fiddle and guitar; where do we take it from here?"

That sort of decadence is characterized not just by malaise and futility but also by substitutes of what we might call "revival," semblances of a returning vitality. The demand for a kind of "revival" societally can provide a powerful draw for demagogues. Steve Bannon, one of the most Machiavellian populist-nationalist entrepreneurs of this age, told an interviewer that he learned his craft from the multiplayer online games industry, and makes his point through a hypothetical man: Dave from Accounts Payable, in the days after his death. "Some preacher from a church or some guy from a funeral home who's never met him does a ten minute eulogy, says a few prayers. And that's Dave," this strategist said. But online, in the world of the game, Bannon says, Dave is not "Dave from Accounts Payable" but "Ajax." He's tough and warlike; maybe he dies in the throes of battle. When Ajax dies, in the fantasy, there's a funeral pyre and thousands of people are there to mourn Ajax the Warrior. "Now who's more real?" he asks. "Dave in accounting or Ajax?" This figure soon realized that the comments section of extremist political media could become more of a community for a certain kind of angry, lonely person than "the town they live in, the old bowling league." That comments section "could be weaponized at some point in time," he notes. "The angry voices, properly directed, have

---

*Ross Douthat, *The Decadent Society: How We Became the Victims of Our Own Success* (New York: Simon & Schuster, 2020), 8–9.

---

latent politics power." The end goal? "I want Dave in Accounting to be Ajax in his life."*

There's an old word for this: *paganism*. Paganism, after all, demands the sort of significance that is heroic—in which one's virtues of strength and power are celebrated in story and song. Joseph Campbell famously popularized Jung's idea of the "heroes journey" a half century ago, but the quest for an imagined heroism is even stronger, and often much, much darker now. Part of the problem, for Dave from Accounts Payable is right there in the description. In an age in which one's worth is often subconsciously attributed to one's status—of income, of education, of position, of "social capital"—can we really be surprised that Dave would want to find some way of being known and loved and seen? And if he can't do that as Dave, is it any surprise that he would try to be somebody else? This ends up in the sort of fantasy role-playing zeal one could see at the Capitol insurrection. Those were real police officers being beaten. Those were real members of Congress being intimidated. That was a real Constitution being threatened. Dave from accounting could be Ajax the Warrior, except that the blood on the floor was *real*. For many of those carrying all this out, it felt like a jolt of life, maybe even like a "revival" of sorts.

Against this sort of lifelessness and decadence mixed with nostalgia, American evangelical Christianity often offers more of the same that the secular demagogues do. Any time and place that's

---

*Jennifer Senior, "American Rasputin," *The Atlantic*, July/August 2022, 26.

not the case, conservative Protestantism offers not revival but revival*ism*. This can be an equally nostalgic and artificial replay of
the entrepreneurial techniques of years past. In some ways, this is
not at all a new concern in the quest for revival. Examining the sites
of evangelical revivals that swept across western New York through
the work of evangelist Charles Finney, historian Sydney Ahlstrom
notes that the "burned over districts" highlighted how religious ex-
citement "had a way of producing its opposite: disappointment, dis-
gust, remorse, ennui, and even a sense of betrayal."* Like addicts
seeking more and more doses of a stimulant to recover the feeling
they had with the first rush of the drug, these places proliferated
with occultism, mysticism, and even communistic utopian experiments. P. T. Barnum, he of "a sucker born every minute" fame,
exploited the surging desire for "enthusiasm" with his own sensa-
tionalism.† Just as with the stimulant addiction, though, the result
was exhaustion and numbness. "Revivalism" itself—when disconnected from authentic revival—can make the situation worse and
not better after all the tents have been taken down, all the sawdust
swept up from the floor.

And yet.

Contrary to some critics of revivalism, of the Left and the Right,
the decadence of "burned over districts" is not the whole story, or

---

*Sydney E. Ahlstrom, *A Religious History of the American People* (New Haven:
Yale University Press, 1972), 476–77.

†Ibid., 488.

even the majority report, of what happened in revivals, many of which resulted in genuine "awakenings," complete with sustained planting of churches. Whatever evangelicalism is, one common factor is an emphasis on the possibility of revival. Evangelicalism sees itself to be, after all, a revival movement in the broader Body of Christ. That sense of the possibility of revival is what has united Calvinists such as George Whitefield with Arminians such as John Wesley, and it's what often defines or redefines a generation—as in the "Jesus movement" among the unlikely mission field of the hippies and surfers during the Vietnam War era. As with the altar call we discussed earlier, "revival" can mean a mechanized, manipulated marketing campaign—or it can mean something the Scriptures speak often about, the power of God in stirring a community—and not just an individual—from death to life.

Evangelicals—along with other Christians—often point to the account of the prophet Ezekiel standing over a valley of disconnected skeletons and being asked, "Can these bones live?" (Ezek. 37:1–14). The answer from the prophet is, "Lord, you know." The mystic imagery of the revival of Israel does indeed happen, and happens in precisely the way we see it happen over and over again in the Bible—through Word (Ezekiel is commanded to "prophesy" to the bones) and through Spirit (the breath of God reassembles the rattling bones and gives them the life to stand as an army). The result of that revival is a new unity—what seem to be irreparably divided kingdoms repent of sin and find their identity under the kingship of the son of the House of David (Ezek. 37:18–28). This is still, maybe even more than in years past, a worthy goal.

To get there, though, evangelical Christians in this time of confusion and disorientation must discern what precisely it is that we are seeking to "revive." If that is merely the nostalgic restoration of some previous (and mostly imaginary) golden age of Christian influence and morality, then no revival is possible. An alcoholic cannot heal simply by imagining the gauzy days of his or her youthful sobriety. He or she must ask what about that sobriety led to the drinking in the first place. The goal is not to "get back" to something but to seek renewal for the future, a renewal that might have continuity with the past but will often look strikingly different from it.

In lasting revivals of the past, the revivals are never a replay of what had gone before, repeating the same methods and propping up the same institutions. Nor were any of these revivals the sort of "modernizing" theological pivot that some on the Left often propose, that Christianity must "change or die" by moving beyond the "outdated" fundamentals of the faith. Revivals are paradoxically disruptive of the present while in continuity with the past. For all the ways that the evangelical emphasis on the Protestant idea of the "invisible church" can degenerate into the sort of anti-institutionalism that can turn Christianity into an ideology rather than a locally lived *life*, key aspects of this model have proven vitalizing and regenerating of actual church structures. Those finding connection beyond their church and denominational borders often are able to return to their own communities with a renewed vision for what's possible for the future, that the decline of existing churches or networks need not be inevitable. At the same time, genuine revival has always come through and after a time of intense disorientation and even what seems to be a tearing-down of the status quo.

The late evangelical leader John Stott once wrote that those who look at the Body of Christ are often, like biologists categorizing species, divided into two categories: "lumpers" or "splitters." The difference is between those who tend to group organisms or people based on their similarities and those who emphasize the distinctions and differences. "Yet both processes become unhealthy if they are taken too far," Stott counseled. "Some Christians go on everlastingly splitting until they find themselves no longer a church but a sect. They remind me of the preacher described by Tom Sawyer who 'thinned the predestined elect down to a company so small as to hardly be worth the saving.' Others lump everybody together indiscriminately until nobody is excluded."*

There are aspects of evangelicalism that are, indeed, obsessed with constant splitting and narrowing. The danger, though, is that people rightly concerned with unity—whether national unity or church unity—will find their quest for such ironically fueling the division. Sometimes unity becomes a way to appease the loudest and angriest voices while silencing those who have no voice.

---

*John Stott, *Evangelical Truth: A Personal Plea for Unity, Integrity, and Faithfulness* (Downers Grove, IL: InterVarsity, 1999), 9–10.

That's especially true when the "unity" we seek is not really cath-
olicity but "bigness." Elected officials pay attention to groups that
are large and can be the deciding factor in swinging elections one
way or the other. A politician in Massachusetts has to march in the
Saint Patrick's Day parade in Boston in a way that one in Camden,
Arkansas, just doesn't. A politician in Utah or Idaho pays attention
to the pronouncements of the Quorum of the Twelve Apostles of
the Church of Jesus Christ of Latter-day Saints, while politicians in
Vermont might well not even know what that is. For evangelical
Christians particularly, an identity politics of "bigness" and "unity"
has not been uniformly good for us. In many ways, it was always
illusory. Christian organizations would constantly threaten to boycott corporations who threaten our "values." In most cases, peti-
tions asking people to hold a chain store accountable for some
moral infraction or other was in most cases just a fundraising mail-
ing list racket for the "pro-family" coalition outfit sending the peti-
tion out. In the moments when this sort of influence could actually
be tested, the results revealed far less influence than that boasted
about by those leading the campaigns. In the 1990s, the Southern
Baptist Convention voted overwhelmingly to boycott the Walt
Disney Corporation because of the allegedly corrupting influences
of Disney on the culture. Baptists, they said, were going to "send
a message to Mickey." The boycott did precisely *nothing* to hurt
Disney's market power, even among Southern Baptists themselves.
When conventions would be held in Orlando, Southern Baptists
walking through Walt Disney World would look down to pretend

they didn't recognize each other, in exactly the old joke said about the way Baptists react to one another in liquor stores. In truth, most evangelical Christians simply are not waiting for their leaders to tell them what to buy or for whom to vote. At least in the latter category, it is usually the other way around. The grassroots coalesce around a candidate or a cause, and the "leaders" compete to show the grassroots how they have been leading them in this direction all along. The claim, though, that we are forty or fifty million strong—and that we are unified—can go a long way in a world defined by statistical success. The kingdom of God is, as I learned to sing in Sunday school, "deep and wide," but such depth and wideness, when sought on its own terms, often leads to hubris or to despair, or to both.

The answer to this "bigness" complex is not the opposite. Smallness and decline do not, by themselves, make things better but in many cases make the situation worse. That's especially true when the expectation or aspiration to bigness is combined with the reality of decline. Speaking of the stagnation of the Catholic Church in America, buoyed for a time by increasing immigration from Catholic-heavy Latin America, Ross Douthat argued, "In a smaller, weaker Church, the influence of ideas that seem weird to the average Catholic today are likely to be magnified, as the Church becomes more an institution by, for, and of the weirdos."* That's a

---

*Ross Douthat, "Catholic Ideas and Catholic Realities," *First Things*, August 2021.

good thing if by "weirdos" we mean "fools for Christ," in the sense of the Christians most committed to the "strangeness" of the gospel in our culture, who are, like the first Christians, deemed "odd" by those around them for not surrendering to the idolatries and immoralities of the age. This, though, is not what I sense Douthat means by "weirdos." This definition sounds like a very close parallel of what US senator Ben Sasse (R-Neb.) meant when, at a speech at the Ronald Reagan Presidential Foundation, he said, not of the church but of American civic life: "This is a government of the weirdos, by the weirdos, and for the weirdos. Politicians who spend their days shouting in Congress so they can spend their nights shouting on cable, are peddling crack—mostly to the already addicted, but also with glittery hopes of finding a new angry octogenarian out there."

We see the fractures facing not only American political life but also virtually every business, church, denomination, neighborhood association, and even family. And in almost all those settings, someone will inevitably ask, "How did we become so divided?" followed by "How do we get back to unity?" Those are important questions, but there are good and bad ways to answer them. Some people will use metaphors such as the Tower of Babel, the biblical account of people attempting to build a tower to heaven, whose languages were altered so that they could not understand one another. But this metaphor often misses the fact that, in the Genesis account of Babel, the problem wasn't the fragmentation; it was the unity.

The confusion of the languages and the dispersal of the people was not a natural by-product of their situation or even of their actions. *God* did it.

As we will see time and again, both in Scripture and in the history since, God often tears apart the unity of the people . . . in order to form a unified people. After all, unity around the wrong things is no real unity at all. The scattering of the Babel builders, after all, is a prelude to what immediately follows: the call of Abram (soon to be called Abraham) out of Ur. Oddly enough, God promised Abram *exactly* what the text said that the builders wanted: a great name, a unified family, a future of blessing. It is through Abraham, the Bible says, that all the nations would be unified and blessed. But if unity alone were the goal, God could have left them alone. The pattern, though, was one of order followed by disorder followed by a reordering. In the New Testament, the great undoing of Babel is seen at Pentecost, where people from all over the world were gathered and, when the Spirit was poured out, started to hear the message, each in their own language.

Pentecost brought about unity, but it was a unity that kept ratcheting up the tension. The same Simon Peter who preached about the Spirit poured out on all flesh would soon face a crisis when Jesus appeared to him to tell him that the Gentiles were joint heirs with him, and that he shouldn't call unclean what God had pronounced to be clean (Acts 10–11). As the Spirit moved outward— from Jerusalem to Samaria to the ends of the earth, each stage created a new crisis. What should we do with these controversial outsiders who have received the same Spirit as we? (Acts 10:44–48). Even that would lead to a series of other crises—Peter had to face confrontation by Paul when Peter avoided eating with the Gentiles in Galatia (Gal. 2:11–14). Peter's motive was, in his own mind, no doubt "unity." If Peter had stuck with the custom of separate tables for the in-group and the out-group, there would have been no tension. The people with a (literal) "place at the table" would never have raised a question, and those harmed wouldn't have been heard from at all. Paul recognized this, though, as not in step with the gospel and withstood Peter to his face. That was fragmentation. Two pillars of the church at odds with each other! But that was the reverberation from Pentecost. God was keeping his promise that "the blessing of Abraham might come to the Gentiles" too (Gal. 3:14). This was not a Babel-like unity, though. This was something quite different. This was God coming down, not humanity building up. God was fracturing the community in order to create a new one—one in which, "Here there is not Greek and Jew, circumcised and uncircumcised, barbarian, Scythian, slave, free; but Christ is all, and in all" (Col. 3:11). This was revival, not reconstruction.

A remnant is usually the way that God brings about revival. He usually pares a people down, clears away the field, prunes the branches, and then starts again. But a remnant without revival is just a demographic in decline. The pattern is order, disorder, reorder. Like in Ezekiel's vision, dry bones can live. But sometimes a field of skeletons is just a field of skeletons. For all the flaws of the evangelical emphasis on revival, the beauty of it is that it, first of all, doesn't give up on the possibility of God acting. God can do a new thing. But also the revival emphasis, while corporate, retains the sense of the personal. "Lord, send a revival," the old song goes, "and let it begin with me." For a cynical people in a cynical time, what seems possible is simply the continuation of whatever trends we see in front of us right now. Revival reminds us that this is not always so. What if the current tumult all around us at this moment is not the evangelical movement imploding? What if it's instead God tearing the evangelical movement down? If so, perhaps we should ask why before we ask what's next. For those of you who are committed to staying with Jesus, and with his bride the church, you can see something of the why already. What's next? I don't mean what's next for the church, much less what's next for American Christianity. You can hardly, on your own, do anything about that. So what can you do?

Embrace New Communities and Friendships. Not long ago, I came across a very conservative evangelical critique of the women's Bible teacher Beth Moore. While this evangelical offered appreciation for the ministry and wisdom of Beth Moore, he suggested that she was a "gateway drug" to feminism, to the erasure of any distinctions of what he believed to be a biblical calling of only qualified men to serve in the ordained pastoral role, and, while she did not hold that office, this evangelical man believed that her ministry blurred those lines in wrong ways. I rolled my eyes and exhaled when I read this critique. It was as arrogant as it was mistaken. Ordinarily I might not dwell much on the musings of some young firebrand with whom I disagree, but the redness on my face in reading the critique was not from anger but from blushing. The evangelical critic was Russell Moore, circa 2007.

I remember those days well. I remember how, as a seminary professor and out on the church speaking circuit, I would often be asked about Beth Moore—who was then, as now, one of the most popular writers and speakers in the evangelical world. I would often preface my response with, "Well, she's my mom and I love her . . ." I did this because I could see the blood drain out of the questioner's face as he (and it was always "he") had the word "Moore" flash across his face. I would then, of course, say that I was kidding and move on. My wife, Maria, would often say at that time: "She is nowhere near old enough to be your mother." This is, of course, true, but the joke landed better with "mom" than with "sister" or "cousin." So I kept doing it for a while, even though, as I often have to say these days, we are of no relation. But, looking back now, I can see that the assumption behind the question—and my answer—was that Beth Moore was not "one of us"—the theologically rigorous "confessional" tribe. She was, I guess I assumed, a "pragmatist" or "seeker sensitive" or maybe even as some called her a "mystic." But I really did not know Beth Moore until two world-shaking realities came to define much of my world: Donald Trump and church sexual abuse. She and I saw these things much the same way—and both of us were, I think, surprised to see that so few other people did. And so we found ourselves in the same orbit, and came to know each other. And, through that, I came to see that Beth

Moore was no "theological lightweight," but that I was. She was supposedly a mystic. That wasn't, and isn't, true—unless by comparison with the sort of proposition-by-proposition hyperrationalism in which any mystery short of a syllogism is suspect. When the night of the soul turned dark for me, I needed that sort of "mystic" much more than I needed an inquisitor. And it's a good thing, because they were almost all gone.

The people who were there for me—for counsel, for prayer, for encouragement—were largely not the people who had loved me for my communications savvy or my writing ability or my confident quipping in conference settings or my résumé or my "future potential." Those people were distant—waiting to see how "toxic" I would turn out to be, whether those who said (laughably) that I was a Marxist would be able to drive me away. But a woman I had been taught to dismiss as a mystic and a lightweight never left me alone. She was constantly checking in, calling and texting Bible verses, praying with me in person or over the phone. She was able to call me back to what I believe—and more to the point, to *Who* I believe. And she could make me laugh, to stop taking myself so seriously. She was no pragmatist. She stood by her beliefs when others vilified her. She was no lightweight. She pointed me to the weight of glory just beyond the horizon. And then I stood back up. I reclaimed my sense of mission and purpose. But I didn't stand up by myself. There were a lot of Aarons and Hurs—and Miriams and Priscillas— holding my arms up. She was one of them. When asked about her, I started saying, without irony now, "She's my sister and I love her."

Revival in Scripture and in history, from Pentecost on, always upends the definition of the pronouns *we* and *us*. Immediately after Pentecost, the church—including the apostolic pillars therein—is rattled by the realization that the mystery of the gospel always meant that the Gentiles—even the despised Samaritans—would be joint heirs with Christ, fellow citizens in the kingdom of God. In a crisis, a movement often is challenged to ask what previous alliances were indeed what evangelicals might call "fellowship," and which were something else altogether. "What we see at the moment is the philosophy of materialism—of the Right, the Left, the Center—at war with itself," Lionel Trilling wrote in the context of the World War II upending of the old international order. "In that war many of our old notions have become inadequate and many of our old alliances inoperative."* Maybe a similar moment is afoot now. Just as countless friendships were broken in the tumultuous years of 2016 onward, some fire-forged strong friendships were created too. Many people were experiencing the exact same realities. Look around for them and cherish them.

What can be true of you personally is also true of what it seems God is doing on a larger scale. Many of the old alliances and coalitions are fracturing. Part of this is because of how the issues to be emphasized by some of the coalitions were chosen and maintained. This can happen with any subgroup of any religion, but I saw it up

---

*Lionel Trilling, "T.S. Eliot's Politics," in *The Moral Obligation to Be Intelligent*, ed. Leon Wieseltier (Evanston: Northwestern University Press, 2000), 22.

close with my own "tribe" of "neo-Reformed" evangelicals. When some were convinced that certain aspects of feminism were out of step with a biblical teaching of important distinctions between men and women, the emphasis was written into numerous creeds and confessions of groups and coalitions. Many of those old controversies were polarized by "slippery slope" arguments. What many of us never realized is that every side of an issue has slippery slopes and if one only sees one of them, one is probably sliding down another. Even more, organizations were formed to "defend" this viewpoint. Very quickly, such organizations needed to justify their existence and began to view almost every issue through the lens of gender. Whatever one thinks about debates over women in ministry or "traditional gender roles," one can hardly conclude that this teaching is a major theme of Scripture, especially when subjects the Bible *does* emphasize repeatedly (baptism and the Lord's Supper) are considered "secondary issues" that rarely cause more than a brief academic discussion or informal teasing with each other between those on the "same side" who disagree on them. One could hardly conclude that a secondary issue is God, but that turned out to be the case. When key leaders justified their "complementarian" views of male headship with positions such as a rejection of the eternal generation of the Son and other aspects of Trinitarian dogma, those deviations were tolerated as "inside the camp," while orthodox, evangelical, conservative Christians who disagreed on whether the Bible limits the pastoral office to men, or who argued that Ephesians 5 taught a "mutual submission" between husband and wife, were on the "outside." There was no culture war over the Trinity or God, but there was one on gender, which made the latter feel more important for definition. And so a group started to see as the "enemy" anyone who deviates on that one matter, no matter how relatively minor, and as "ally" anyone who agrees. That's how we end up with statements demanding churches that have women serving in pastoral positions of any kind be kicked out of denominations with biblical references to 1 Timothy 2, by men who, as everyone close to them knows, violate the 1 Timothy 2 command for men to avoid quarrelsomeness, and who do not themselves meet the 1 Timothy 3 qualifications for deacon, much less pastor. And it's how you end up with situations in which defending human slavery, employing vulgar and shockingly sexist language against women, and covering up for sexual abuse mean that we can "make room" for such a leader in the tent, while excluding a humble, godly leader who believes the Bible teaches that "election" is based on God's foreknowledge of human choices, not on his unconditional decree. This is twisted, and it twists us. It does not have to be this way.

Maybe you're a complementarian (someone who believes that some pastoral positions are only for qualified men), and you are looking around to see that some of those you thought were with you on theological grounds were actually just misogynistic. Maybe you're an egalitarian (someone who believes all gifts and offices are open to both men and women) but are realizing that you have more in common with someone who disagrees with you on some texts but affirms both the authority of the Bible and the value of women and girls than you do with the person who, yes, believes in the ordination of women but thinks that the apostle Paul was himself a misogynist or that the use of "Father" and "Son" language is sexist. Maybe you're an Arminian who finds that you have more in common with a Calvinist friend than you do with someone else who emphasizes human free will to the point they inadvertently adopt some form of Pelagianism. Maybe you're a Calvinist who realizes that you have more in common on the sovereignty of God with an Arminian friend than you do with the people who seem to see predestination as just one more way to "own the libs" by sending them to hell. In all these cases, you might find that you feel closer to people who differ with you on a secondary matter but who share the same motivation. Maybe sometimes you will find that people who differ on an "end" but who agree on the "ways and means" to get there can be unified more easily than when it's the other way around. Some of our differences are really important. You aren't resolving not to ever argue. You are resolving *how* you're going to argue later—and what kind of people you will be when you show up to do so. Pay attention when you see God doing that.

Moreover, notice that the places where Christian revival fires seem to be burning in the world are far away from anywhere where George Whitefield or John Wesley ever preached. The next Billy Graham quite likely not only did not vote for or against Donald

Trump, but as likely also doesn't speak English. Even in a time when "globalism" is derided by populist movements of the Right and of the Left, it just might be that American Christianity can find more in common with one another across the world than we can sometimes find next to us in the pew. And it just might be that, in so doing, the least "catholic" wing of Christianity might rediscover the immediate force of the words, "I believe in the Holy Spirit, the holy catholic church, the communion of saints." White American Christians are actually *not* a "moral majority" or a "silent majority" or any majority at all, unless we define our primary culture as that of the United States of America. If, instead, our first identity is part of the global Body of Christ, then white middle-class Americans are a tiny sliver indeed, and the driving force of Christian orthodoxy and spiritual energy in the world, and even in the United States, is not white and middle-class. And where there is evangelistic energy within American evangelicalism, such is often centered in immigrant churches, whether Dominican or Cambodian or Nigerian or Iranian.

Pray. This seems like the most routine answer an evangelical preacher could possibly give. And yet I think we pass right over it as though it were obvious, especially in a time when "thoughts and prayers" in the public arena is just a way of saying, at best, "I care about you," and, at worst, "I am not going to do anything to help this bad situation." Even within the church, "I'll pray for you" can easily be a stand-in for "I care about you," the equivalent of saying "Call me if you need anything" to someone who's just lost a parent or a spouse. We say it because there's nothing else to say. By "pray," I mean, to *really* pray. Revival starts, as with Ezekiel, first with the taking in of the reality of an army that is vast but dead, and thus hopeless. Almost no set of "techniques" for bringing about church revival will ignore the need for prayer. But prayer cannot be simply another technique. As with an individual sinner, the stirring of a community to new life starts with an acknowledgment of powerlessness, of ignorance, of a lack of a clear strategy at all. That's because prayer itself can only be offered that way; faith itself can only grasp on to gospel reality that way. A person who loves an institution—or the theology or the history or ideals behind that institution—will often start mistrusting his or her own gut and intuition that is saying something is really wrong. In any institution, one can start to think that the very fact that everything seems normalized means that the one seeing the craziness of it all must be the crazy one. Maybe stop fighting the loneliness and desperation of it all and instead let it prompt you.

Prayer starts, by the Spirit, with what the apostle Paul compares to a baby screaming in anguish to a parent (Rom. 8:15). Often in such prayer, the apostle teaches, one will not know what to pray at all, "but the Spirit himself intercedes for us with groanings too deep for words" (Rom. 8:26). We need this because any quest for renewal must start with hope, and the Bible teaches us that hope is for that which is unseen, not that which we can see or simply a return to what we have seen before (Rom. 8:24–25).

During the Keswick Convention revival movement of the twentieth century, the phrase "Let go and let God" became popular to the point of cliché among those in the Deeper Life movement. This slogan, and the underlying theology beneath it, were critiqued harshly by many in the more doctrinally robust wings of evangelical Christianity, as presenting an unbiblically passive view of how a person is to pursue holiness. The criticisms were usually right—identifying an overreaction to what Keswick preachers saw as exhausting, "works-based" attempts at fidelity. And yet, while the "Let go and let God" formulation is not *enough* to encompass what the Bible describes as the life of faith and obedience, the slogan is certainly right that this is where all faith and all obedience must *start*. Jesus taught that one must first "hunger" and "thirst" for righteousness—that is, identify a lack, and then seek to find a source to fill that lack—before one can find it (Matt. 5:6). The disciples of Jesus all had plans and strategies—all of them ground apart by the events of the arrest and crucifixion. After they were thrown into confusion and close to despair, Jesus told his followers not to strategize but to *wait*—for the Spirit to fall at Pentecost.

This stance runs counter to our ambient marketing culture, inside and outside the church. Institutions and communities aren't supposed to admit that they can't fix things. That, we are told, looks weak. This is especially true in an American Christianity that brings "can-do" entrepreneurialism to everything from world missions to Bible translation to church-planting. But part of the rage that we see against institutions all over the world right now is a reaction to the sort of grandiosity that offers the illusion of solving any problem and meeting any need, even the needs for transcendence and meaning. When these expectations aren't met—as they never could be—the consequence is a disillusioned and increasingly angry public, resulting in political and social and religious movements led by those who would channel the anger of the people, lie that they alone could fix the problems, and then disappoint, starting the cycle all over again. All of that ends in nihilism.

Our best option at this point is to lose our stability in order to find it. The nostalgia some of us feel for an old sense of order and predictability and influence is not in and of itself wrong. If we pay attention to it, it can tell us something. The poet David Whyte argues that nostalgia is not always delusion or indulgence. "Nostalgia tells us we are in the presence of imminent revelation, about to break through the present structures held together by the way we have remembered," he writes. "Something we thought we understood but that we are now about to fully understand." He concludes, "Nostalgia is not an immersion in the past, nostalgia is the first annunciation that the past as we know it is coming to an end."* Or at least it can be. Don't try to come up immediately with a strategy, whether that's to deal with your own distress and disillusionment or to "save the soul of American Christianity." If you do that, you will probably end up "reviving" the wrong thing, and will miss out

*David Whyte, *Consolations: The Solace, Nourishment, and Underlying Meaning of Everyday Words* (Langley, WA: Many Rivers Press, 2016), 151–52.

on what's genuinely renewal, revival, rebirth. Sometimes you need to spend some time sending out the messages in bottles. That can be hard until you find that there are really people out there on the other side. Maybe we need to do more than just play the old hits, and assemble focus groups with our present audience. Maybe it will take some outlaws to get on the Damascus Road again.

CONCLUSION

The scary thing about an altar call is that you don't know where you are going. Of course, at the literal level you do, at least if it's an actual old-fashioned altar call. You're walking forward. Maybe you see someone standing there, smiling, ready to receive you. But you don't really know where you're going. I didn't. When I walked down the aisle to profess faith in Christ, as a little Southern Baptist kid in Mississippi, I knew I loved Jesus and I wanted to follow him the rest of my life. But could I really have imagined what that would mean? When I walked that same aisle again, to tell my church that God was calling me to ministry, how could I have known what kind of a world I was stepping into? What if a time-traveler were there, stopped me in the aisle, and said, "Let me tell you about evangelical Christianity several decades from now. Let me tell you about Donald Trump. Let me tell you about ongoing racism and nationalism constantly trying to masquerade as Jesus. Let me tell you about all the people whose faces you will see the rest of your life, people who were violated at the deepest core of their being, by the church." Would I have listened? Would I have turned around and headed back to my pew, or would I have kept going right through the foyer and out the back door? I don't know. Who can know? Altar calls, literal and metaphorical, are first steps, first steps on what's meant to be a pilgrimage.

Whenever we are worshipping in a different church, my wife will put her hand on my back if the hymn "Come Thou Fount of Every Blessing" starts to be sung. That's to remind me not to wince if the worship band gets rid of Ebenezer. The lyrics of the song include the line, "Here I raise my Ebenezer; hither by thy help I'm come, and I hope, by thy good pleasure, safely to arrive at home." This is always the part people want to skip or, worse, change to something else. The rationale is, "Nobody knows what 'Ebenezer' means; they think it's the name of a Dickens character." I will always respond, "That's my point! How are people to learn the stories if we do not tell them, and sing them!" Many people don't know who Abraham was either or, for that matter, what a more abstract concept such as "grace" really means. But I always stop myself, because I know I'm yielding in those moments to my inner curmudgeon, and I probably sound like the Grand Ole Opry star in the rhinestone suit deriding how the outlaws were ruining everything.

"Ebenezer" is important, though. Ebenezer is a monument, a "stone heap" marking where God delivered his people from the

Philistines and, more importantly, recovered the Ark of the Covenant, the central locus at the time of God's presence with Israel. The prophet Samuel set up the monument and called it "Ebenezer" because "Till now the LORD has helped us" (1 Sam. 7:12). Monuments are important, and they are all over the biblical story. When the people of God came into the Promised Land, stones were set up on the banks of the Jordan through which they passed, so that when future generations ask, "What do these stones mean?," their elders can retell the story (Josh. 4:4–9). When you sing a hymn and a child or a new Christian or even a longtime Christian says, "What in the world is Ebenezer?," that's the time to tell the story again. We need those monuments, those markers of what happened in the past, those symbols of stability and continuity. Often these monuments in the Bible are referred to as "pillars." The pillars are standing stones, meant to bear witness to an experience with God—such as Ebenezer or Bethel, the place where Jacob dreamed of a ladder coming down from heaven and laid down a pillar to mark the spot (Gen. 28:18).*

That's why it's confusing to read in the Exodus story of something referred to as a "pillar of fire" and a "pillar of cloud." Instead of a marked, stable monument to an event in the past, the pillar of fire and cloud went ahead of the people, leading them through the waters of Egypt toward the Promised Land, giving them light through

---

*"Pillar," in *Dictionary of Biblical Imagery*, ed. Leland Ryken, James C. Wilhoit, and Tremper Longman III (Downers Grove, IL: InterVarsity, 1998), 645.

the nights and a canopy of protection through the days (Exod. 13:21). The people followed this pillar out of the land of slavery. And when the people were, from there, trekking out into the wilderness, this pillar of fire and cloud took up residence with the people, in a movable tent called a "tabernacle," a kind of portable temple. When the cloud was on the tabernacle, the glory lighting it up, the people would set out. And when the cloud would disappear, they would stop, and wait (Exod. 40:34–38). Notice the mysterious paradox of the pillar of fire and cloud: it was both an illuminating fire and a darkening cloud. There was both direction and mystery. And maybe even more confusingly, it's called a "pillar." This was no monument. This wasn't stable but moved. This couldn't be set up by a group of people or torn down, or even approached.

Philosopher Leon Kass explains how significant it was that the people would reassemble this Tent of Meeting at each stopping place, and that the cloud would reappear, showing them which way they should go. "Unlike the fixed palace of an earthly monarch, the portable Tent of Meeting moves as the Lord directs," Kass argues. "As he is not bound to a natural place or to a manufactured residence, so his dwelling place, like the people who built it, moves after him." And, unlike the nature gods of the people around them, Kass contends, the appearance of the cloud, the pillar of fire, could not be predicted by any rhythm. When it appeared, they went forward; when it disappeared, they waited: "He moves not in circles but toward a goal."* This pillar didn't point to the past but led out into the future, into the unknown.

This distinction between pillars, between a monument and a manifestation, even confused the closest followers of Jesus. The Gospels refer to a mysterious moment when Jesus led Peter, James, and John up on a mountain and was "transfigured" before them. He was lit up with a supernatural light of glory, and the site was over-shadowed with a cloud. Peter wanted to pitch tents, to tabernacle there. He wanted a kind of monument. But the glory would not be contained, and wouldn't be bound or predicted or placed (Mark 9:1–8).

Scary times almost always evoke nostalgia in some and resent-ment in others. In frightening times, someone will always be there promising a way to "get back" to what we once had—and it doesn't matter if "what we once had" is defined as "the Lost Cause" or "Make America Great Again" or "Revive Us Again." Christianity, though, doesn't move into the future that way. In the Chronicles of Narnia, when the children asked the professor about how to get back to Narnia, he told them that the wardrobe through which they had entered was not a portal they could control. "You won't get into Narnia again by *that* route," he said. "Indeed don't *try* to get there at

---

*Leon Kass, *Founding God's Nation: Reading Exodus* (New Haven: Yale University Press, 2021), 586–87.

all. It'll happen when you're not looking for it."* Jesus never promised, contra conservatism, a golden age in the past, at least not within human memory. And he never promised us, contra progressivism, a golden age in the future, at least within human possibility.

You need both kinds of pillars, but you must not confuse the one for the other. In your own life, there are, no doubt, "pillars" that point you backward, reminding you of what God has done before and what he can do again. You need that. Those are reassuring and give us the confidence to keep walking. The pillar of fire, though, is scary. It points you onward, and, like your ancestors in their journey, it gives you only enough light to see just ahead. You will see that the light goes out into the wilderness with you, but often these times will feel to you confusing and disorienting. You will feel lost. Only in retrospect, if at all, will you see what God was doing. The temptation at the moment, though, will be to pitch the tent in place and look to the pillar of memory rather than to follow the pillar of glory. The light is there, though; the cloud is overhead. Moreover, this pillar of glory is not really a "thing," but a person. Where it is pointing you to is the final New Jerusalem, which has "no need of sun or moon to shine on it, for the glory of God gives it light, and its lamp is the Lamb" (Rev. 21:23). The Lamb *is* the Light. The pillar of fire and cloud still leads on.

The gospel of John tells us that, in the middle of a crisis threat-

---

*C. S. Lewis, *The Lion, the Witch, and the Wardrobe* (New York: HarperCollins, 1950, 1978), 188.

ening his life and safety, Jesus returned back to where he had started his public ministry, back to the Jordan, where John had baptized him. This was where once there was a pile of stones marking the God who kept his promise to bring a people safely through water. That sign was gone now. Jesus was there in what must have seemed like a retreat, a momentary withdrawal from the bedlam back in the inhabited places. And yet, many people drew to him there, the Bible tells us, and they said of the baptizer, "John did no sign, but everything that John said about this man was true" (John 10:41). John did no sign—nothing miraculous or extraordinary or strategic or world-shaking. He just pointed. How the people discovered that he was telling the truth was to find Jesus for themselves, to do what Jesus repeatedly said to those who would follow him, "Come and see."

One Sunday morning I stood on the platform of our new church, over a horse trough filled with water. In the middle of all this, my son Jonah, then fifteen years old, the same age I was when I went through, and emerged from, my adolescent crisis of faith, professed his faith in Christ. He asked to follow Jesus in baptism. His baptism was not like mine was, in this under-ten-years-old church-plant with no baptistery, no organ, no white robes. But as I raised my hand and heard myself saying, "In obedience to the command of our Lord and Savior Jesus Christ and upon your profession of faith in him, I baptize you my brother, in the name of the Father and of the Son and of the Holy Spirit," I realized that his baptism was, in all the important ways, just like mine. My home church wouldn't have known or claimed the word *evangelical*, but that's what we were. Much of what they told me wasn't true. And that's hard for me to face, even now. As Frodo Baggins said, "I feel as long as the Shire lies behind, safe and comfortable, I shall find wandering more bearable: I shall know that somewhere there is a firm foothold, even if my feet cannot stand there again."* Much of what they assumed turned out to be, just what I feared, a mixture of southern honor culture, American patriotism, Republican politics, white racial backlash, and on and on. If I don't face that squarely, I cannot be honest with myself or with you.

But everything they told me about Jesus was true.

The novelist Frederick Buechner wrote that it is as impossible to prove the existence of God "as it would be for even Sherlock Holmes to demonstrate the existence of Arthur Conan Doyle." Instead, he wrote: "In the last analysis, you cannot pontificate but can only point. A Christian is one who points at Christ and says, 'I can't prove a thing, but there's something about his eyes and his voice. There's something about the way he carries his head, his hands. The way he carries his cross. The way he carries me.'"† In Jesus, we encounter what all of us intuitively know to be true—that there is a vast unseen mystery that holds the universe together. We find

---

*J. R. R. Tolkien, *The Fellowship of the Ring* (Boston: Houghton Mifflin Harcourt, 1954, 1994), 61.

†Frederick Buechner, *Wishful Thinking: A Seeker's ABC* (New York: HarperCollins, 1973, 1993), 36–37.

someone who answers our deepest longings—including the need for guilty consciences to be at peace. The apostles spoke of this as "the Mystery of Christ." And Buechner reminded us that, in following that sort of Christ, "you do not solve the mystery, you live the mystery."* The stories are true. The tomb is empty. The women in the garden weren't lying. And if you ask me how I know that, I might start out with all the philosophical and theological arguments I've learned to give, but then I would stop and simply say, "Come and see." And that's why, if you happen to be at my funeral whenever in the future it happens, you'll notice that what the people gathered there are singing is the same invitation hymn I heard so many years ago—"Just as I am, without one plea, but that Thy blood was shed for me, and that Thou biddest me come to Thee—O Lamb of God, I come, I come." And when you hear it, you can know that I would walk that aisle all over again.

John the Baptist did no sign—and the Baptists who raised me didn't either. People around Jesus kept asking for signs. And he said that no sign would be given except the sign of Jonah. "For just as Jonah was three days and three nights in the belly of the great fish, so will the Son of Man be three days and three nights in the heart of the earth," Jesus said. "The men of Nineveh will rise up at the judgment with this generation and condemn it, for they repented at the preaching of Jonah, and behold, something greater than Jonah is here" (Matt. 12:40–41). That's it. That's the sign. The sign is the

---

*Ibid., 76.

scandal of a cross—of a Messiah who would bear the shame of execution by Rome, who would offer his own blood for the reconciliation of God with the world. And the sign would be that the most pagan godless, morally decadent, ruthlessly violent society imaginable—Nineveh—would see a defeated, beleaguered, half-dead prophet and believe that what he was saying was true. What Jesus didn't mention is that the prophet Jonah didn't like the repentance of his enemies. He wanted God to be a manifestation of his own tribal resentments and nationalistic passions. He wanted revenge. He wasn't just fish vomit—he was disobedient, compromised, and immature.

"And many believed in him there." That's what the Bible tells us about those crowds who followed Jesus back to the Jordan. Not all of them, but many of them believed. That's the sign. As I pulled my own Jonah up out of the water of that horse trough, I realized that his baptism is far more similar to most of the church than was mine. In creeks and riverbeds and barrels and swimming pools, people around the world are still hearing that same message—that God so loved the world that he gave his only begotten Son, that whosoever believes in him should not perish but have everlasting life.

American Christianity is in crisis. The church is a scandal in all the worst ways. We bear responsibility for that. Some of us contributed to it. Some of us were crushed by it. We cannot will it away by shrugging our shoulders and saying, "That's just the way people are." But however many hucksters and grifters lead this movement, sinners still find in Jesus someone who is not. No matter how many people wave "Jesus Saves" signs over their atrocities and insurrections, that doesn't stop the fact that, well, he does. Evangelical Christianity as we know it might not survive. American evangelicalism might not be there for the future. But someone will be. As long as there's a church, there will be people within reminding everyone else that the Spirit blows where he wills, and that there's hope, no matter how far gone a person goes, to be born again. There will be those people who will remind the rest of the church to search "the Scriptures daily to see if these things [are] so" (Acts 17:11). There will always be those people standing around rivers or streams or horse troughs or space pods, reminding everyone else that there is still power in the blood. I'm counting on those people being there. And who knows what they will call themselves. But for now we might as well call them "evangelical."

You might be more than skeptical. Like Nicodemus, you may ask, "But how?" And perhaps Jesus is saying to us, "The wind blows where it wishes, and you hear its sound, but you do not know where it comes from or where it goes" (John 3:8). Like Thomas of old, you and I might ask in exasperation, "Lord, we do not know where you are going. How can we know the way?" And perhaps what Jesus is saying to us is, "I am the way, and the truth, and the life. No one comes to the Father except through me" (John 14:5–6). Maybe when we're blind enough, we will be able, once again, to see the pillar of fire out there in front of us. The challenge before us is not to "Make America Great Again" but to "Make Evangelicalism Born Again." And that's not a strategy. That's a prayer. Maybe when we're lost enough, we can re-find the Way. Maybe all the dangers, toils, and snares are worth it. Maybe only when we lose our religion will we be, once again, amazed by grace.

Acknowledgments

This book could not go out into the world if not for the wisdom, skill, and leadership of Bria Sandford, editorial director of the Sentinel imprint at Penguin Random House, who gave innumerable hours to shaping and reshaping this book, and to my literary agent Andrew Wolgemuth, who led in this process from the very beginning.

This book would not exist without the readers of *Christianity Today* and of my weekly newsletter, where I worked out the "first draft" of many of the thoughts and ideas here. The questions and responses of these thoughtful people guided me to this point. I am also indebted to my colleagues at *Christianity Today*, especially Christine Kolb, Timothy Dalrymple, Erik Petrik, Mike Cosper, and Joy Allmond.

I am hard-pressed to describe the depths of my gratitude to my team at the Ethics and Religious Liberty Commission (2013–2021), a band of brothers and sisters who excel in skill but also and more importantly in love, joy, peace, gentleness, kindness, goodness, faithfulness, and self-control. This includes especially Phillip Bethancourt and Daniel Patterson, to whom this book is dedicated. A recounting of their courageous leadership and Christlike conviction would take up a book of its own (and one day might). They knew not only how to do things but also how to stand—on the truth of the gospel, on the way of the Spirit, and on compassion for the vulnerable. I am also grateful to the board of the ERLC, who likewise demonstrated love, bravery, grit, and Christ-shaped conscience. That's especially true of my former chairman of that board, my friend David Prince, about whom I could also write a shelfful of books and still not adequately describe my thankfulness.